David Bennett

exploring concrete architecture

Tone Texture Form

Birkhäuser – Publishers for Architecture
Basel · Berlin · Boston

We would like to thank the
following institutions who kindly
sponsored this publication.

Aalborg Portland, Aalborg, Denmark
British Cement Association, London, United Kingdom
Bundesverband der Deutschen Zementindustrie e.V., Berlin, Germany
Eerste Nederlandse Cement Industrie
Febelcem, Brussels, Belgium
Instituto Español del Cemento y sus Applicaciones, Madrid, Spain
Irish Cement Ltd., Dublin, Ireland

Graphic design: Alexandra Zöller, Berlin

This book is also available
in a German language edition.
(ISBN 3-7643-6270-7)

A CIP catalogue record for this book is available
from the Library of Congress, Washington D.C., USA

Die Deutsche Bibliothek – CIP Einheitsaufnahme
Bennett, David:
Exploring concrete architecture: tone, texture, form/David Bennett –
Basel ; Berlin ; Boston : Birkhäuser, 2001
Dt. Ausg. u. d. T.: Bennett, David: Beton
ISBN 3-7643-6271-5

©2001 Birkhäuser – Publishers for Architecture,
P.O. Box 133, CH-4010 Basel, Switzerland
A member of the BertelsmannSpringer Publishing Group
Printed on acid-free paper
produced from chlorine-free pulp. TCF ∞

Printed in Germany
ISBN 3-7643-6271-5

9 8 7 6 5 4 3 2 1   http://www.birkhauser.ch

Contents

Preface

Modern architectural concrete can be engineered to be more responsive to structural forming and sculptural shaping than ever before. The many bold and vibrant examples on the use of concrete in this book confirms the belief that architects have learnt from the lessons of the past and are sensitive to the inherent properties of modern concrete. It remains to be seen whether the creative architecture reviewed in this publication can in time be as influential as the concrete achievements of the great Pier Luigi Nervi's Palazzetto dello Sport in Rome, Robert Maillart's Salgina Gorge Bridge, Berthold Lubetkin's High Point 1, Eero Saarinen's TWA Terminal at John F Kennedy Airport, Oscar Niemeyer's Government Buildings in Brasilia, Erich Mendelsohn's De La Warr Pavilion, Le Corbusier's Villa Savoye or Félix Candela's shell roof structures.

Exploring Concrete Architecture highlights the current vogue amongst European architects for expressing the functional and decorative potential of concrete in buildings and public spaces. It describes how the individual architect has interpreted spatial and sculptural form and exploited concrete's visual qualities; sometimes it has been juxtaposed in stark contrast with other materials like glass, steel and wood; sometimes it has been left as struck with 'warts and all' to reveal the formwork indentations and construction marks; sometimes it has been painted to act as a canvas; sometimes it has been point-tooled and diamond-polished to expose the beauty of the aggregates and reveal the true colour of concrete.

Each of the 22 project documentations provides details on the material choices, the surface finishes and construction approaches taken and about what was intended, what was achieved and how well it worked. It considers both the architect's and contractor's viewpoints and expresses them candidly. The opening chapter reviews the key aspects on successfully specifying architectural site cast concrete. The author is indebted to Aalborg Cement (Denmark), BCA (UK), BDZ (Germany), ENCI (Holland), Febelcem (Belgium), IECA (Spain) and Irish Cement (Ireland) for sponsoring the visit to each country to meet the architects and contractors involved. Individual thanks go to Jef Apers of Febelcem, Hans Köhne of ENCI, Christian Justesen of Aalborg, Jörg Fehlhaber of BDZ, Julio Vaquero Garcia and Sergio Carrascon of IECA and Colm Bannon of Irish Cement for their considerable help in arranging the visits and to Martin Clarke of the BCA for championing the sponsorship that ensure this book was printed in colour. I would like to dedicate this book to my partner Jennifer Crossley.

High quality, well-finished site cast concrete has been the ambition of many architects, bridge engineers and contractors the world over. Cast in place construction rather than precast concrete, so the theory goes, can also be a competitive cladding option as it offers greater construction efficiency, and a reduction in cost. But the reality is that many architects and their clients believe that trying to achieve a precast finish using site cast concrete is just not feasible. Why?

On the whole not many architects are prepared to specify cast in place concrete because they do not have confidence in the building industry to produce good visual concrete. On many occasions the production of fair-face site cast concrete has been a catalogue of remedial work, contractual losses and client dissatisfaction. Architects who have attempted to specify fair-face concrete have been appalled by the poor performance of the construction industry, more pre-occupied with volume business rather than quality. Who is to blame? The architect for not understanding that concrete has a skin that breathes, soaks up moisture, attracts dirt and pollution and weathers just like stone, or the material technologists and the construction industry for not formulating additives and surface treatments that could minimise the effect of weathering?

Experienced contractors complain that architects are not giving them the proper guidelines in the contract on how to achieve the fair-face work specified nor the colour that is wanted, other than a very subjective description. More often than not, the contractor will price for something less than the architect has envisaged for the work, and when that happens the kango hammers and variation instruction start flying. Is there a solution?

For a few years now, it has been heartening to hear and see evidence that concrete in architecture is gaining recognition as a material full of sculptural and economic possibilities – another word for inexpensive – in the UK. It is architecturally well respected and better understood in Switzerland, Scandinavia, Holland and Italy probably because the construction industry in these countries have good concreting skills. At a seminar on concrete, British architect Piers Gough entertained, illuminated and gently teased the concrete die-hards in the audience on the art of his bespoke architecture and how combinations of mass and minimalist expression can work well together with concrete. Here is an architect who admitted to being ignorant about the 'good news' of insitu architectural concrete, but who was willing to test its possibilities on one of his future projects. Gough ranks among the most creative and eclectic designers when it comes to residential apartments, private houses, public and community buildings with projects such as China Wharf, Cascades Aztec West and Westbourne Grove to judge by. Yet Gough's candour hinted that architects may be guilty of largesse with the brief when it comes to specifying insitu concrete, as they must rely on the integrity and good will of the contractor to get it right – and that is one reason not to specify it!

It was Ray Emery, Area Technical Manager for Pioneer-Willment Concrete in Shoreditch, who poignantly brought home the problems handicapping the ready mixed industry, regarding architectural concrete specifications. 'It's just like a crisis facing Ford Motor Works, after they received an order to built a Ferrari on the same assembly line turning out Escorts and Fiestas by the hundreds every day', explains Emery. The ready mixed industry are the Fords of the construction world, a volume business and not many specifiers – be they engineers, contractors or architects – fully appreciate that. 'We have frequent requests for prices for special architectural concrete – it's usually a shade of white – and we fight the same uphill battle of being given too little information to work with, and too little time to help the client and the project team save money', says Emery. In the architect's eye a precedent has usually been set for a particular white, be it from a Dulux type colour chart or a picture in a book, but usually there is no description in the specification to achieve it other than 'it shall be white'. On one occasion, Ray Emery recalls with a chuckle, when an architect was asked to be specific about a shade of white, he grabbed a sheet of copy paper from a photocopy machine and said 'make it photocopy white!'

The point that Emery was making was neatly summarised from a series of trial mixes he had made. They were all shades of white or grey-white concrete. Each laboratory mix had the equivalent of 400 kgs of cement, with an aggregate cement ratio not exceeding 6:1 and a water-cement ratio of 0.40. The water-cement ratio controls the intensity of colour for a particular cement content – the higher the water content the lighter and less intense the colour, and visa versa. The 400 kg cement content ensure a uniform saturation of surface colour, providing enough cement particles in the mix to fully coat the fine sand particles and aggregates. So it was important to keep these two factors constant.

In combining these materials to produce the various shades of white or white-grey, the cost of ready mixed concrete production, according to Ray Emery was as follows:

MIX A: White
White Cement, Ballidon Aggregate, Hepworth Sand price £ 260/m^3
MIX B: White
White Cement, Marine Coarse Aggregate, Hepworth Sand price £ 180/m^3
MIX C: White with hint of sand tint
White Cement, Marine All-In Aggregates price £100/m^3
MIX D: Light Grey with hint of sand tint
GGBS/OPC, Marine All-In Aggregates price £ 50/m^3

The reason for the large variation in cost, above the differences in material costs, is that in producing Mix A for example, three bins have to be manually cleaned out, washed and made ready for the cement and the two special aggregates, plus allowances for the consequent loss of volume production for small quantities. Mix B requires two special bins and Mix C one special bin to worry about, hence the proportionally greater drop in the price. Whilst Mix D is made from materials in every day use at the ready mixed plant, and produces a uniform light grey coloured concrete.
Now the architect should be asked the question what shade of white do you think the client will pay for? Early discussion with a ready mixed supplier will bring greater understanding and certainty in the drafting of specifications for the supply of ready mixed architectural concrete. And it must be treated as a separate item with

quality control based on maintaining a fixed cement content and water-cement ratio, not a strength criteria. Not many specifications are written with that in mind. In short, many architects stay clear of site cast concrete and only specify precast concrete. But precast production output is limiting, it is expensive and heavily reliant on cranage. Can the quality of site cast concrete be improved?

In Search Of Good News

It's a hot July day, and with hat and camera, sitting half asleep, half awake, I was enjoying a slow burn on the deck of a river boat with a garbled commentary about Chicago's famous buildings, when suddenly ahead I saw a smooth, curved, grey white building standing quite alone on the water's edge. The building was Bertrand Goldberg's River City Plaza, the architect who designed Marina City and unashamedly admired the work of Le Corbusier. The building facade looked crisp, clean and smart, no tell-tale rust runs or pockmarked in-fills to the fair-face concrete finish. It was ten years old and I was looking at the finest cast in place high rise structure ever built in recent decades. So what's the story, how did Goldberg achieve what no one, apart from Tadao Ando or Peter Zumthor, has consistently done since?

The answer according to Symons Corporation of Chicago – who supplied the formwork package, the form liners, the release agents, and the upward pumping method on River City Plaza – was ensuring that the contractor adhered to the specification and workmanship techniques that were stipulated by Symons for architectural concrete. 'Invariably when we find there are problems on one of the jobs we have supplied with an architectural concrete package, it has been because the contractor has decided to skip or compromise on the procedures that we have laid down', says Ray Bartholomae, General Manager of Symons Corporation. 'We are able to offer a guarantee to the client and architect that a good visual concrete finish can be achieved every time, if our procedures are followed. We have not lost a case against Symons on that point.'

The concrete for producing good architectural concrete, whether it is cast in place or precast, briefly must have the following characteristics :

— *Cement content must be in excess of 350 kgs/m³*
— *Aggregate-cement ratio must not be greater than 6:1*
— *The sand should be a zone M to BS882*
— *Water-cement ratio should not be greater than 0.5*
— *Formwork and release agent that will produce blemish free surface finish*
— *Release agent and any admixture in concrete must be compatible*
— *Constant high frequency poker vibration should be used*

The Right Mix

To ensure that the concrete colour is consistent and uniform from one batch to the next, the cement content must remain constant, the source of the cement must not change and the water cement ratio must remain tightly controlled with the minimum of variation. The colour of concrete is controlled by the finest particle in the mix, which is usually the cement, and any sand particles finer than 150 microns, unless a pigment is introduced which is finer. The paste that forms on the face of the concrete in contact with formwork is a mixture of cement and pigment, if included, sand and water; with the cement and pigment dominating the colour. If however the water content changes, then in areas where the water content is higher the concrete tone will be lighter and where it is lower, it will be darker in tone. Tests for conformity of concrete production should be based on cement content checks and water-cement ratio measurements and not cube strength. There are techniques and simple testing equipment for monitoring these properties quite quickly on site.

Formliner manufacturers like Symons of USA, Noe of France and Reckli of Germany may not agree with Tadao Ando on the most cost effective way of forming architectural concrete, but how Ando achieves good insitu concrete finishes is worth noting. 'In civil engineering the concrete used is very hard, giving the impression of being very powerful and strong. I insist on using hard concrete which is the final finish. We use plywood for formwork and then varnish all the panels to ensure a good surface to receive the concrete. In Japan we have a tradition of highly skilled carpenters and joiners and these craftsman help to create aesthetically finished exposed concrete', explains Ando.

On Goldberg's River City Plaza – built in 1986 – the whole structure was cast in place using a modular formwork system which was lined with an elastomeric formliner. The concrete was placed by upward pumping into the storey-high façade forms. The formliner and specially formulated neutral non-staining release agent ensures that the concrete is uniform in colour and does not suffer from surface discoloration during compaction and when the formwork is removed. Upward pumping avoids any trapped air getting into the mix, when concrete is placed in the forms. The pumping action of the concrete also helps to remove any large air pockets in the mix. Frequency of vibration and poker size is checked for the radius effect of poker vibration to determine the ideal spacing of the poker and the depth of immersion into the concrete. This will ensure that vibration is the same intensity on the face of the forms. This is a critical procedure for architectural concrete and one that is often overlooked in most concrete specifications.

Chemically neutral non-staining release agents or specially formulated wax emulsions are important in good visual concrete production. Trial formwork panels should be cast to check the compatibility of the release agent and the forming surface. Very dense forming surfaces like metal and plywood panels with a heavy duty overlays, usually a bonded phenolic resin film, will give a shiny surface finish with a tendency to highlight and exaggerate small tonal changes in the colour of the concrete. The advantages with such systems is that they can be re-used fifty or more times. On the other hand to produce a matt surface finish, it is best to use a plywood with a medium density overlay, usually a resin impregnated film; which will also reduce incidence of blowholes and tonal variations but will have only ten re-uses. High density plastic formliners with a cheap formwork backing and the correct release agent, or a good birchwood-ply coated with polyurethane paint and sanded to give a smooth, matt surface finish would be a viable alternative for multiple uses.

Tadao Ando suggests rubbing down the surface of the concrete after the formwork has been removed and when it has hardened sufficiently. This process will smooth over minor blemishes and take off any surface discoloration, but it may not be necessary if the correct formwork and release agent has been used. It is a hugely labour intensive operation that will create a lot of dust and may not be appropriate for countries where labour is expensive.

It is vital to consider the long term effects of weathering, moisture staining, and lichen growth on concrete, which has a porous and absorbent surface skin. Coatings which blend well with the natural look and colour of concrete, that are not shiny nor turn straw colour or break down in UV light, should be prescribed to make the new concrete surface impermeable. Recently the National Theatre in London, that masterpiece of concrete architecture designed by Denys Lasdun in the 1960s, has had a much needed revamp by architects Stanton Williams. New bars, books stalls and lifts have been installed, spaces within the building have been opened up and the dirty facade given a good clean at last. It is a great building whose only flaw was to have left the exterior board marked insitu concrete finish without a barrier coat to prevent moisture ingress and dirty staining. Now that been put right, the 'National' is going to find many more admirers amongst young architects.

Adventures With Concrete
Several architects in the past two decades have taken a serious interest in the development of visual concrete. In the case of Riccardo Bofill's Taller de Arquitectura, concrete is used as the primary material for their monumental neo-classical designs. The ability to mass produce precast panels with such fine detail can be put down to the understanding of the mouldability and flexibility of insitu concrete, of its innate colour when pigmented and textured when acid etched, grit blasted, stained or waxed. To keep the cost down on Bofill's early social housing projects, both the monumental precast pieces and the ashlar concrete wall panels were cast on site. Nowadays with his reputation well established, clients are prepared to pay for factory produced precast panels using a technique called 'shocked concrete'. This entails lifting the concrete mould a few centimetres and dropping it about 100 times per minute. This produces a dense low porosity concrete which can be used for finely detailed finishes.

In John Outram's eyes concrete has always been an expressive material, not a monochrome, cool, grey stone. His design fragments solid colours into heavy precast tiles of 'nougat' concrete, creating a carpet of floating colour and contrast. Many of his designs are so intricate and complex that they can only be fixed by stone masons, a tile at a time, and are hugely labour intensive and costly. This does not make it conducive to factory fabrication nor efficient assembly on site. Perhaps such bespoke exclusivity in concrete does not make the ideal role model for young architects to pursue. On the other hand the architectural practice of MacCormac Jamieson Prichard (MJP) have been very successful in adapting designs in precast concrete for large panel assembly, bringing together many contrasting, highly enriching textures in concrete, wood and glass. For the Fitzwilliam Chapel College in Cambridge for example, a hierarchy of materials have been explored – precast concrete and rendered insitu concrete, integrated with American oak, and veins of brick courses in displays of exquisite craftsmanship. Every part of the chapel has been detailed and built with an intense striving for perfection. Here the idea of using concrete as a high quality interior finish, in the fashion of the National Theatre, is executed with the finesse of a cabinet maker. When you have a substantial budget for a building, it is easy to design and detail such exotic concrete. Perversely that's why the LSE Student Accommodation Building was chosen ahead of other MJP projects, as it shows just what can be achieved with precast concrete working to a very tight budget under the constraints of a design and build contract. For even greater flamboyance and expressive architecture without pretension, the precast detailing of CZWG's Cochrane Square has much to admire.

There are many architects represented in the book who prefer the smooth, minimalist monotone grey of concrete, with no surface texture, no bush hammering, no nothing – just mass, solidity and neutrality. Real concrete to them is 'as struck' concrete, transparent in honesty, a man-made stone whose monolithic form works well in combination with glass, steel and wood floor finishes. When the conservative city of Osnabrück invited Daniel Libeskind, a radical modernist architect, to design a new wing of a museum dedicated to the art of Felix Nussbaum, the news was first greeted with surprise. Nussbaum was on the last train to Auschwitz in 1944, where he was to die in the gas chambers. Nussbaum was a Jew who painted with vivid colours and loved sunflowers just like Van Gogh, an artist he is often compared to. In his last years Nussbaum's paintings were of death, the horror of Nazi oppression, and scenes of a life devoid of culture, art and joy.

For the new museum Libeskind has created a powerful, uncompromising vision of the artist's life and works. The building that he has designed is divided in three parts, each wing forming the side of a hidden triangular courtyard. Each wing is built with different materials to represent the different aspects of the artist's life: wood for normality, zinc for the future and concrete for exile, the holocaust and death. The tall thin spine of the concrete wing, with its bare, bland walls of insitu concrete is meant to depict a blank canvas. It's a disturbing and disorientating experience, which Libeskind has handled with cleverness and understanding of both material and subject. Concrete here has been used as pure material and an art form, and it has worked extremely well. The Arken Museum of Modern Art by Søren Robert Lund, the Crematorium in Berlin by Axel Schultes, the Moebius House by Ben van Berkel and Morella School by Carme Pinós and Enric Miralles, share the same aspirations.

The perceived view of concrete as the unsightly brutalist material of the 1960s can no longer hold true for the pragmatic 90s. Whether a concrete has been cast in place or precast, whether it is smooth or point tooled exquisitely like the House in Constance by Christoph Mäckler or left deliberately raw with dark patches and blowholes to provide a dramatic contrast with machine fabricated material or gunited with red pigment over the whole façade of a building; clearly from the projects reviewed in this publication there is a revival in the expressive potential of concrete and a growing enthusiasm to work with modern architectural concrete. What is now sought is a collective wisdom from these and other experiences, to share knowledge and understanding in order to improve and refine the process of cast in place production.

A Guide to Specifying Visual Concrete

These notes have been prepared from direct experience and research on visual concrete production, the information collected from the projects highlighted in this book and research on concrete finishes published by the Concrete Society in the UK in 'Technical Report 52'. They have been drafted assuming British Standards.

It is important that the ready mixed concrete supplier is involved early in the discussion on the choice of concrete colour and finish, to check availability of cement types, availability of special aggregate or pigments, and to agree on a practical and affordable concrete mix that can be supplied to the project. Consult with formwork, formliner and release agent suppliers to determine the best product(s) to achieve the required surface finish. Impart this information clearly and concisely in the specification to help the contractor to understand and price what is required.

Seek advice from the research and marketing division of the cement and concrete industry in your country. It is usually free.

The Concrete Mix

Concrete mix constituents shall be weigh batched and truck mixed generally in accordance with BS 5328 or European equivalent.

The proposed concrete shall comply with the requirements for fair face concrete work viz. cement type and content, pigment, water-cement ratio, aggregate and sand content and not a strength criteria. The concrete mix in combination with the formwork and selected release agent – when properly placed and compacted – will produce a blemish free finish, free of blowholes and give a uniform surface colour appearance.

The proposed concrete mix shall be cast in a sample panel to prove the integrity of the concrete mix, the formwork system and workmanship in meeting this requirement.

For general guidance, the proposed concrete mix should comply with the following characteristic to satisfy uniformity of colour and surface finish.

1. The concrete workability shall be sufficiently cohesive for vibrator compaction, pump delivery, handling by conveyors and chutes on site, to free fall 2 m, and to be placed in vertical forms without segregation or causing excessive bleed water to rise to the surface.

2. The concrete must have a cement content not less than 350 kgs/m³ and must be taken from the same batch of cement to eliminate possible changes in cement colour. State what cement type is required – white cement, light grey GGBS cement or grey Portland Cement and describe what colour the concrete is required to be.

3. The type of cement, cement content, water-cement ratio, fine aggregate content less than 150 microns, pigment concentration and any approved admixtures shall be fixed for all concrete supplied to the contract and must not be adjusted at any time during the contract. Fine materials of particle size less than 150 microns control the surface colour of concrete. Pigments are the finest

particles followed by cement and a small proportion of sand than is smaller than 150 microns.

4. The water-cement ratio shall not exceed 0.5. Once the ratio has been agreed by the architect following successful trial mixes and panel construction, it must not be adjusted at any time during the contract, as any variation in the total water content will effect the surface finish colour.
5. The total aggregate-cement ratio shall not exceed 6.
6. The sand-cement content shall not exceed 2. The sand should be a zone M or similar type sand without too much fine dust. Sand content expressed as a percentage of the total aggregate by mass should not exceed 40%.
7. Coarse aggregate 20–5 mm: not more than 20% to pass a 10 mm sieve.
8. Any plasticiser, water reducing admixtures or pumping aid used in the mix must be stated and their compatibility checked with the release agent. Some admixtures can react with release agents to create gas bubbles and this could lead to entrapment of blowholes on the concrete surface.

Production Quality Control

Truck delivery tickets must show the batch weights of all mix constituents, including the total water content and total water-cement ratio and show compliance with the approved mix constituents. They shall be given to the concrete contractor for recording and checking on arrival on site. If no delivery ticket is presented, the concrete shall be rejected.

Concrete shall be sampled from the truck mixer before discharge and slump tested to check the colour and uniformity of mix. If any noticeable colour variation is evident, then the concrete shall be rejected.

Accurate weigh batching and control of aggregate moisture content is essential in the production of good visual concrete. Store aggregates under cover in bins to prevent rain wetting stockpiles. Monitor moisture content of aggregates regularly and adjust free water content to maintain the correct water-cement ratio.

Wet batched concrete is preferable to dry batched concrete, as it eliminates the variability and uncertainty of truck mixing efficiency. Some trucks are not efficient concrete mixers, they can only agitate the mix because of the paddle configuration in the mixing drum.

Concrete Placing and Compaction

Clean and wet concrete skips, conveyors and any other concrete handling plant before use.

Remove all discharge of grout in the pumping line and excess water as pipeline is primed.

Place the first layer of concrete into position across the whole length of the formwork for a wall pour and roughly tamp to level. If necessary, use the poker to melt the top of high points in the layer before commencing poker vibration. The maximum depth of an uncompacted layer of concrete shall not exceed 500 mm. High frequency immersion poker vibrators shall be used with the right diameter to effectively vibrate the concrete to the full width of the form or the distance to the outside form face. The spaces between vibrating points shall ensure that the cone of vibration of the last position just overlaps the next vibrating position. The rate of concrete placing shall be uniform and must exceed 2 m/hour in vertical sections.

Prior to commencing the work, the contractor shall be required to produce a sketch drawing of the pour planes and poker immersion points for a typical column and wall pour. This is necessary to show that the type and size of poker, and its radius effect of vibration will adequately compact the concrete layers and maintain an even compaction force at the form face, to ensure a consistent concrete colour. If the compaction on the form face varies greatly then this inadvertently causes dark and light colour variations to appear on the finished surface.

Use rubber linings over vibrating pokers for all compaction work to slab soffits. Do not use the poker vibrator to move concrete into place. Tremie or chute the concrete into positions for the vertical forms to avoid concrete splashes to the form face or segregation on the rebar, before it reaches the bottom of the pour. Spade the concrete near to the formwork face to release any air pockets. Do not place poker vibrators near the formwork face. This will avoid poker burns and noticeable variations in colour and aggregate density on the exposed concrete face.

Revibration

Revibrate concrete at the top of the vertical pour after 1-2 hours to eliminate potential colour banding due to excess bleed water rising to the surface.

Surface Tolerances

a) Abrupt changes to formed surfaces: a max. deviation of (2 mm) is permissible between formwork panels.

b) Formed surface imperfections: blowholes are permissible up to a max. size of (3 mm); their number may not exceed (10) in any square metre.

c) Floor surface finish must be smooth with no abrupt changes. Variation in level must be not more than 5 mm in 3 m, in any direction.

   ( ) modify figures according to required quality.

Formwork

a) *Grout Tight Joints:* The formwork shall be grout tight and all joint between panels sealed with an appropriate sealant to eliminate grout loss. The formwork and tie bolts shall be designed to resist a full liquid head, and high amplitude vibration during compaction and must not deflect more than 1/360. To prevent grout leakage at tie bolt holes, use plastic snap-tie cones with rubber gaskets on the tie.

b) *Release Agent:* Use only neutral pH, non-staining release agents which when applied to the formwork will not wash off during rainy weather. It shall adhere to the formwork and debond the concrete effectively while the forms are in place (up to 36 hours) without causing blemishes, discoloration or blowholes to form on the surface finish or later cause the surface to dust. Evidence that a proposed release agent complies with this requirement must be proven.

c) *Construction Joints and Panel Layout:* Rebates shall be formed at concrete construction joints to form a neat edge to the construction joint. The position and detail of all construction joints shall be shown on the contractor's falsework drawing, together with a layout of formwork panels and tie-bolt hole positions for approval by the architect, prior to the commencement of concrete work.

Formwork Striking Times: Formwork should be stripped about 24–36 hours after casting. This will give a consistent colour to the concrete and avoid exposing the forms to prolonged heat of hydration and chemical action of the concrete in breaking down the release agent. It is important to strip formwork to give the same equivalent maturity time throughout the project as even small variations in maturity time can cause colour variation between panels. Maturity time will be less in hot weather than cold weather, and these times can be evaluated from cement content and actual concrete curing temperature.

Making Good: No making good shall be permitted to certain surface finishes indicated on the drawings. In all other areas making good may be permitted subject to approval by the architect and to a standard that matches the reference panel.

Reinforcement: Supply clean cut reinforcement, with no rust marks, for all exposed concrete work.

Cover and Spacers: Cover to slab and walls shall not be less than durability requirements shown on the structural drawing. Spacers for slab and wall reinforcement shall be of plastic construction, rigid enough to maintain rebar cover without deformation and small in contact area with formwork to avoid marking the exposed concrete face.

Curing: Direct wet curing of concrete or wrapping concrete in polythene sheeting is not permitted, as this will cause dark and light patches to form which may not fade in time. Maintain a small but definite air space between any impervious protection such as polythene or tarpaulins to avoid direct contact with concrete. Curing membranes are not permitted as they will stain and prevent any coatings bonding to the surface. It may be best to do nothing if after removal of formwork the surface has hardened sufficiently and will not dry out prematurely and become dusty.

Reference Panel: The reference panel should be a full storey high and bay width panel. If form liners are used the panel should be at least two liner panels wide to observe the vertical joint. The finished result should be a true reflection of the quality of the workmanship, curing and construction method.
Formwork, formliners, mix design materials, release agent, concrete handling and compaction procedure and the actual operatives that will be deployed on the job should be involved in casting the panel. Patch repairs of blowholes (should that be permitted), location and filling of tie-bolts holes, and such like should be evaluated and agreed at the same time. If the surface it to be rubbed, etched, mechanically abraded and/or coated with water repellent covering to eliminate dirt staining or water absorbency then this treatment shall be carried out.
In this way the quality of the finish can be agreed, highlighting areas for possible improvement and setting the standard for the project. The surface finish may include small variations in tone even if the work has been done correctly, but these are likely to be distributed randomly over the whole surface rather than being concentrated in one spot.

Consideration should be given to a sensible viewing distance for the reference panel, as scrutiny from close quarters would be unreasonable unless particular sections of work merit such inspection. In this event consideration should be given in the contract bill to prepare and cement wash the concrete face to produce an even blemish free finish, if that is what is desired. This is a very subjective judgement as the projects in this review have highlighted. Most architects have preferred to leave the surface untouched, to show the natural grain of minor imperfections – the blowholes and blemishes – rather than cover them with a veneer of cement slurry or cement wash which make the surface look painted and plastic.

Quite often the finish tone of grey or white concrete can become an issue, because the architect or client is undecided on the final colour. There is no definition by which the quality and colour tone of the finish can be unequivocally described by specification alone. The same concrete mix poured into different formwork or placed in the same formwork at different temperatures, or retained in the forms for different length of time will result in colour variations. The longer the concrete is cured or left in the forms the darker the surface tone. The lower the water-cement ratio the darker the tone. It would be prudent to conduct colour sample trials with the concrete supplier making concrete cubes or small panels of concrete, prior to commencing expensive, full scale reference panel.

Compliance
Having verified to the architect or his/her representative that concreting procedures have been carried out correctly, the concrete supplied is to specification, formwork panels cleaned and prepared and removed diligently, taken every care to maintain the same quality of workmanship as the reference sample with no change of site operatives, then the resulting concrete finish shall be deemed to satisfy the specification, provided that a) blowholes are less in diameter than the specified maximum and number less than the number specified per square metre and match the reference panel; b) there is no honeycombing from grout loss or the like; c) the blemishes to the surface are no worse than the reference panel; d) alignment and surface tolerance are within specification; e) making good where permitted brings the surface finish to within compliance standard. Otherwise the concrete shall be rejected and the work redone.

Social Science Faculty Centre and Library, Oxford

Foster & Partners

As you approach the top of Manor Road by car in Oxford, heading towards St Catherine's College playing fields, the long grey structure of the new Social Science Faculty passes you by. From the outside, the building looks like a giant lunch box with windows, its plainness and lack of decoration alleviated only by the asymmetry of the storey-high glass panels – some white, some clear. Step inside and it is a cathedral of natural light. The neutral grey of the insitu concrete columns, the floor slabs, the ceilings and shear walls, and the huge clear glass panels create a sanctuary of light, reflection and calm. Here is organic architecture tempered by structural discipline with the simplicity of a framed concrete building, common to so many two-storey buildings and yet it says much, much more.

Location

The building is situated in the north-eastern corner of Oxford, along Manor Road which is a turn off Long Well at the St Cross Library Building.

Design

The building has been built to a very tight budget. Insitu concrete was the preferred choice and given the right team to build it and the programme incentives, the scheme could be achieved with the quality of finish that was wanted at the keenest tender price. The first phase to be completed has a net floor area of 3,500 m² spread over three floors. The ground floor houses the central library of the faculty, the first and second floor accommodate the cellular study rooms for the lecturers and researchers, the administrative offices, the plant rooms and lecture theatres. The design of the building allows visitors and building users the opportunity of experiencing views of the wooded stream and meadow beyond the site. Generous natural light is brought into the building by the inclusion of an east–west atrium corridor that contains the central staircase leading to the two accommodation floors, and through a fully glazed triple height circulation area on the ground floor.

The insitu concrete is expressed internally as the structural frame comprising floor slabs, supporting column and shear walls. Externally, slender precast panels have an insitu like finish to cloak the edge of the insitu slabs and perimeter columns. Purpose-made fluorescent light fittings are mounted directly to the underside of the slab for both the open plan spaces and cellular study rooms. Translucent and clear glazing panels – arranged in a deliberately random order on the façade to make the building appear longer – enclose the concrete frame and allow diffused natural light to enter the building. The glass façade panels are fitted flush with the precast concrete exterior panels but there is a rebated edge in the concrete fascia which acts as a channel for collecting rainwater running down the glass face to avoid staining the concrete surface. It was a detail that had been observed on the Smithsons' Economist Building in London from 1964 which had weathered extremely well.

The building is ecologically and environmentally sensitive with the services based on a naturally ventilated system with the edge zones of the façade incorporating passive shading devices. Mechanical ventilation systems control the room temperature in the deep space areas and the lecture theatres. The flat roof is an upside down roof with a 25 mm asphalt layer bonded to the con-

Design sketch of lobby area.

Atrium corridor and central staircase under construction.

crete slab and then built up with tightly jointed insulation mats, a waterproof membrane and then 70 mm of light reflective gravel which also acts as the drainage layer.

Construction

Architect's Comments: The concrete frame contractor has done the near impossible – constructing a standard concrete frame with very few blemishes. The square columns have neat chamfers on their corners, the shear walls have their bolt holes exposed as though they had been cored by a diamond drill, while the soffit of the flat floor slabs have slight indentations like pencil lines, scribing parallel lines that run on grid lines between columns. We had to make a series of trial panels and mock ups until we all agreed on the concrete mix, formwork panel type and the release agent. But once that was achieved we let the contractor get on with the building, confident in what he was doing. Perhaps that is the point, deciding on the amount of imperfections and slight colour variation that could be tolerated and which inevitably occur with site cast concrete. The ambient temperature of the air, the humidity or lack of it, rain and hail, and the delay before the formwork is stripped can affect the finished colour. While poor placing and compaction technique can exacerbate any minor imperfections in mix design, cause honeycombing and blowholes, or dark and light bands of concrete pour planes due to variations in the water-cement ratio. We were not expecting a paint-like finish to the concrete. It had to have an authentic concrete look, so we accepted it would have a few blemishes, some variation in colour and small blowholes. We did not want the whole surface rubbed up and bagged.

Contractor's Comments: The contract was run as a construction management project giving the architect a hands-on approach during construction, enabling them to work closely with the concrete frame contractor to agree the position of every tie bolt hole, the formwork panel layouts, the location of service holes in the slab for the lighting boxes, and the shadow line rebates in the edge beam and slab soffit and so on. We tried very hard to give the designers the maximum time to develop their designs with the trade contractors without compromising the programme. The formwork for the pile caps was prefabricated and then crane-lifted into place once the formation had been blinded and pile heads trimmed. The substructure and ground floor slab work went like a dream, but we had problems above ground. Almost half of the ground to first floor columns had to be broken out; as fast as the frame contractor was putting them up they were knocking them down! The columns had to be recast because the surface finish was below standard. It was full of large blowholes, because pockets of air had been trapped against the forms. However, this problem did not occur on the shear walls and core walls, which were cast with Visaform shutters. So what was causing it?

The column's metal shutter faces had been grit blasted, and this roughness combined with the stickiness of the microsilica concrete supplied by Tarmac Topmix, was trapping air bubbles against the forms, despite adequate internal poker vibration. We cured the problem by using additional external vibration and by sanding down the metal forms after each pour. By the third re-use the metal shutters were giving the surface finish we wanted.

Detail staircase.

Flush-fitting glass panels,
feature lines indented on
concrete.

Exterior views.

Central staircase.

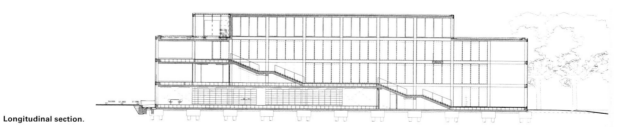

Longitudinal section.

Ground floor.

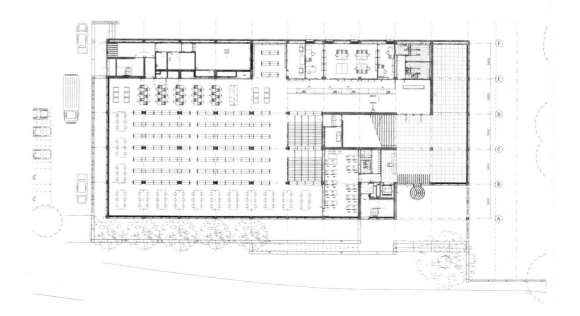

Every last detail has been thought through by the architect, from the lock of the door handle, the computer port on each desk, the flip-up power socket on the carpeted floor below the desk; to the light switches, the ceiling lighting modules, the immaculate plant rooms and water dispersal chases on the slender precast fascia panels. The plant rooms are beautifully laid out. Everything is easily accessed. Its like being on the bridge of a modern ship.

Tolerances for alignment and level on the structure was very strict, for obvious reasons. The structure was the architecture and the finished surface. It was the frame for the doors, the opening for the storey-height glazing units, the surface to fix the lighting modules and switches. The outstanding features of this building are the main entrance with its cantilevered roof propped by a pencil thin column two storeys high, the flush glass and concrete structural line, the luminous atrium and the inspired central staircase.

Architect: Foster & Partners
Structural Engineer:
Andrews Kent & Stone
Services Engineer:
Roger Preston & Partners
Construction Manager:
Heery International
Concrete Frame:
Duffy Construction
Piling: May Gurney
Cladding Contractor:
Harty Holdings
Services Contractor:
Kvaerner Rashleigh
Weatherfield

Project Value for Phase 1:
£ 4.5 million
Net Floor Area: 3,500 m²
Construction Phase:
48 months
Completion: 1999

Main façade – translucent and clear glass panels in random sequence.

Crescent House, Wiltshire

Ken Shuttleworth

Cast in place concrete has been used to form the two crescent walls that run almost parallel to one another, creating the spines of support and the external and internal surfaces for this simple yet imaginative dwelling for an architect and his family. The concrete walls have been painted white to create a strong unifying colour that will reflect light into the house as well as respond to the beautiful chalk hills that it overlooks. Structural concrete was used in the construction of the crescent walls and their foundations. Out of this minimal construction comes an architecture that is immediately accessible and easily understood.

Site plan.

Location

The house is situated on the edge of the Marlborough Downs in the heart of Wiltshire on a five acre site called Winterbrook, not far from the former RAF base at Wroughton. A housing estate lies to the west of the site while to the north there is a concrete batching plant, a sewage works, and rubbish tip. The best views are to the south and east towards the Vale of the White Horse and the Downs.

Design

The concept for Crescent House is not that it should be a modern box artificially placed in a landscape, but a living space that is rooted within its location. The house has been designed as a series of long crescent shaped walls with contrasting sides that are covered by a flat concrete roof. To the north-west the external wall is solid and windowless, shutting out the unwelcome views and the neighbours' prying eyes. To the south-east with its wonderful views of open country, the façade is a transparent wall of glass. Internally the house is characterised by its open plan living spaces. There are few doors. These spaces both absorb and reflect the changing quality of natural light and in so doing create sensory 'walls of contact' with the landscape. All the private spaces – the bedrooms, changing rooms and washrooms – are contained in the fortress like enclosure of the windowless crescent wall which shields the occupants from the prevailing winds and driving rain. These rooms have been designed as small contemplative spaces that are naturally lit from the glass openings in the roof. Here the relationship with the environment is focused upwards at the sky, the stars, the sun and the sound of rain. The decoration is plain. The bathrooms use raw in situ concrete troughs for washing and bathing. All plumbing and wiring is accessible, not buried in the walls or floors. The tendency for architectural indulgence, fussy detailing and designer items has been eliminated.

The south-east crescent is enclosed by a solid inner wall,

Night view of open south-east elevation.

a flat roof and an external glass façade 36 m long and 4 m high that diffuses the barrier between the house and garden, pulling the landscape into the house. The south-east crescent is the garden room which incorporates all the daily family activities of cooking, eating, relaxing and playing. It is the social hub of the house. The garden room and the private sleeping areas are separated by a curving gallery corridor. The double height gallery contains the main entry to the house and the internal circulation. Moving along the gallery, the width reduces until it opens out into the vast garden room with its monumental feature fireplace rising out of the gallery wall. The fireplace is the heart and pivotal point of the

Windowless external wall of north-west elevation.

The garden facing living space.

Garden room and central corridor.

house. Stairs lead to the upper gallery level which houses the library.

The house has been designed to be sensitive to the environment. The whole structure has been externally wrapped in CFC free insulation – 100 mm to the walls and 200 mm to the roof giving the building a very high insulation value. This helps to minimise heating bills, CO_2 emissions and allows the building to remain cool n summer. The house is naturally cross ventilated, with the chimney acting as passive stack for the ventilation system in the summer. The SAP rating is 85 with U values for the roof of 0.2 W/m^{2}K ; 0.3W/m^{2}K for the walls and 1.8W/m^{2}K for the glazing. The building has been designed to receive photovoltaic solar panels to reduce energy running costs, plus rainwater storage and water for washing from an adjacent well.

The quality of the changing natural light has been a driving force in formulating the design. The bedrooms and bathrooms are totally top lit by a long slot formed at the top of the north-west wall. The gallery lighting is from a continuous translucent window. During the day the garden room is lit by daylight entering the full height glass wall, and at night by restrained lighting on the back wall which lights up the curve of the wall.

All the walls and ceiling surfaces of the building are finished in white except the chimneys and shear walls which are left as raw concrete. The floor is carpeted and is grey. Colour is added to the furnishing to represent the changing seasons – blue for winter, yellow for spring, green for summer and red for autumn. Towels, cushions, bed linen, tablecloths, vases and the like are faithfully changed to mark the changing season.

The garden is landscaped to evoke the indigenous flora and character of the Wiltshire countryside and its historical setting. It consists of a wildflower meadow, a woodland of broad leaf trees, grassed walkways, an orchard, a bonfire circle and compost heap contained within a large circle of a hundred maple trees. There is a straight path from the house leading to an existing woodland of mature trees. The house itself is pushed tightly into the north-west corner of the site to maximise the views across the garden landscape.

Continuous window slot lights the gallery.

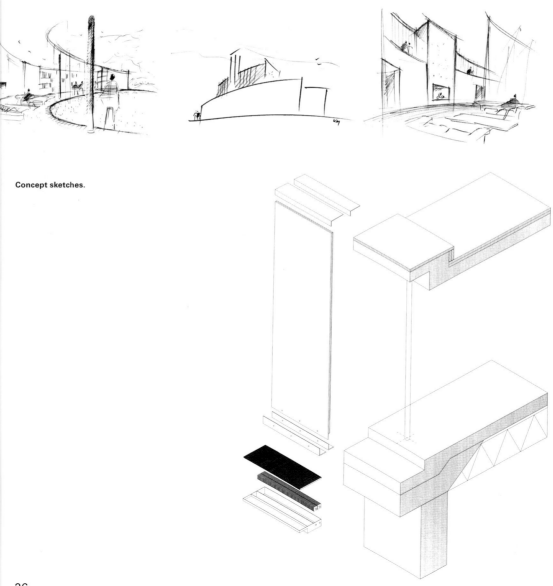

Concept sketches.

Axonometric of structure.

26

White-washed walls and
glass façade of living room.

Closed north-east elevation
facing the main road.

Curving gallery corridor
separating the garden room
from the sleeping area.

Construction

Architect's Comments: The decision to use concrete was
made because of the presence of a ready mixed concrete
plant directly opposite the site. Minimal transportation
of material was therefore necessary and maximum use
was made of local resources. In addition the timber to
shutter the concrete was partially recycled from an old
house and numerous outbuildings that were demolished
on the site, while the rubble was used for backfill.

The roof is a 250 mm reinforced concrete flat slab supported on concrete walls 900 mm long by 150 mm thick
where they could be fitted within the block walls zones.
At the front of the living area the roof slab is supported
on slender, circular hollow steel columns to minimise
obstruction of the view. The roof slab has 200 mm of insulation above it so that good thermal mass and thermal
efficiency was provided. All the exposed concrete was to
be left with a natural 'as struck' finish showing the shutter panel joints, tie bolt holes and surface blowholes. The

Construction of ground floor
columns.

external faces of the concrete walls were covered with
insulation mats that were pinned to the wall and then
rendered. The internal walls were painted white after the
surface had been bagged over and all the blow holes
filled in. The wash basins, shower trays and baths were
made water tight and non-absorbent using a mineral
based paint that closely matched the in situ concrete

Column detail.

colour. The concrete mix designed by Tarmac Topmix was varied for cohesiveness and fluidity in order to place it by pump, barrow or skip. For a 35 N/mm^2 grade concrete, the cementitous content was 210 kg/m^3 of Portland Cement (PC) and 90 kg/m^3 of Pulverised Fuel Ash (PFA) with a water-cement ratio of just under 0.5 that included a plasticising admixture for greater workability. The recycled formwork was cleaned, sanded down and sealed with matt varnish. The curved walls were made simple and robust in construction by adopting the contractors layout for the forming panels and by using small diameter bars to maintain the curving profile of the wall. Nothing was demolished after the walls were cast. The project was organised as a co-operative with everyone contributing to the end result – the contractor and engineer worked together to agree the construction details. Everyone was made to feel this was as much their project as it was the architect's – the work was funded on a time and material cost basis. There was no profit margin and no tender document – the construction details evolved as the work progressed. Everybody looked for ways to make cost and time savings. Conduits, box outs and fixture on the walls were carefully located and cast in with the shutters so there was no chasing out to be done later. The ground floor surface was power floated to receive a carpet to eliminate the need for screeds. Even the kitchen worktop was made of concrete and was hand trowelled to a smooth level finish.

Client: Ken and Seana Shuttleworth
Architect: Ken Shuttleworth
Structural Engineer: Ove Arup
Services Engineer: Roger Preston
Lighting: Claude Engle
Main Contractor: Dove Brothers
Concrete: O'Rourke

Project value: £ 345,000
Construction Phase: 9 months
Completion: 1997

Insitu concrete wash basin.

Roof slab to garden room.

Roof slab over sleeping quarters.

London School of Economics, Myddleton Street Residence

MacCormac Jamieson Prichard

The elevations of bright red brickwork are rhythmically punctuated by recessed window openings that rise past the upper floors in a series of unbroken planes. The window openings are articulated by a symmetrical arrangement of brilliant white concrete lintels, corbels and cornices drawing the eye ever upward to the loftiness of the whole elevation. Around and above the datum established by these focal points, the underlying structure of the building is revealed. The building is an annexe to an existing student accommodation building owned by the LSE. It is hard to believe that such expressive architecture can be built for a knockdown price on such an otherwise uninspiring corner of London.

Location

The 0.1 hectare site is on the corner of Myddleton Street and Gloucester Street in Finsbury, North London and to the rear of the existing LSE student accommodations that front Rosebery Avenue. The site was once a car park

Precast pilasters, corbels, cornices and sills.

and service yard to the existing student building. The ground level of the Myddleton Street annexe is at basement level of the existing block, because the land falls from Rosebery Avenue down towards Myddleton Street.

Design

The LSE's brief required that this building should provide 140 new study bedrooms, and a series of teaching rooms and social function rooms which could also be used for conference facilities with accommodation, outside term time. The income derived from this would be used to subsidise student rents. The floor areas of the new single and double en-suite rooms had to be approximately equivalent to those in the existing building. In line with the LSE's disabled-access policy, the brief demanded five study bedrooms with private bathrooms suitable for disabled students, plus disabled access and w.c. facilities throughout the building.

Rather than provide all the services in a central core, the study bedrooms are grouped in clusters of four around the landings, forming clearly identifiable social units which colonise the common corridors. These landings relate directly to the staircases. The relationship of the window to wall and the window to room layout are varied throughout the building, giving a changing aspect to each room whilst maintaining the unity of the repeating plan. Overlaying the circulation pattern are the two lift cores which are in the corners at the overlap with the taller five-storey residential wings and basement conference rooms.

In order to reduce the school's tax liability, it was decided to build the new wing as an annexe rather than an extension. This entailed the structural separation of the two buildings and no covered access between them. Compared with the unusually high level of domestic and commercial architecture which characterises this area, the immediate context of Myddleton Street is relatively uninspiring. Only the short row of Georgian houses to the south of the site called for any positive response. Thus the massing of the scheme reacts to the bulk of the adjacent hostel and office buildings, while the lower three-storey central block offers a principal street façade which is sympathetic in scale to the terraced Georgian housing further along Myddleton Street.

For security reasons the access is through the reception of the existing building. The lack of a front door led to the

Terrace and bar.

Rhythm of wall and window recesses.

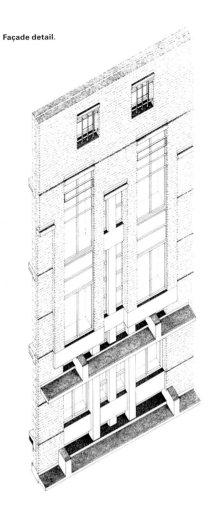

Façade detail.

adoption of a language of fenestration to model the building elevations and to establish a compositional rhythm along the street. The elevations are articulated from pavement to eaves by a series of changes in plane which alters the relationship of the wall and windows. At the base the windows appear as punched holes in a plinth. Above it they are either paired across party walls or developed into a triple form, which sets up a rhythm defining the wings of the building. As they extend up the elevation, the windows appear in relief, encased by brickwork and framed by white precast pilasters, lintels, sills and cornices that reveal the existence of the concrete structure behind them. At the highest level of the building, the articulation breaks clear of the planes of brickwork to form a glazed loggia beneath a deep overhanging, parapet eaves.

The decision at a late stage to let the contract on a design-build tender, with the architect and structural engineer nominated by the client, led to the builder's work details and choice of materials being left more open to contractor preference and interpretation. This approach was largely successful insofar as the building was constructed as drawn, although the role of the architect as design subcontractor left the client sometimes stranded when potential savings and variations were being negotiated.

Myddleton Street elevation.

Inner courtyard.

Client: LSE
Architect: MacCormac Jamieson Prichard
Structural Engineer: RT James
Services Engineer: Zisman Bowyer
Quantity Surveyor: Edmond Shipway
Main Contractor: Laing London
Precast Concrete: Sindall Precast Products

Project Value: £ 2.8 million
Completion: 1994

Construction

Architect's Comments: Precast concrete was specified using a white cement with Derbyshire limestone coarse aggregates from Ashton Keynes and crushed rock fines from the same source. The surface was given a light grit blast which removed the surface laitance without revealing the coarse aggregates, to leave it with a stone like appearance. The panels were designed with drip moulding to the sills and sloping top surfaces to control staining from rain water and weathering. Construction tolerances for precast units were more generous when abutting the insitu frame and more precise when surrounding brickwork. The precast manufacturer was permitted to repair chips or cracks on units provided it was agreed in advance with the architect and provided the unit was not too close to ground level where it could be damaged by vandalism or the repair easily seen. The judgement as to what was an acceptable chip or crack which could be repaired and what was not, was a very subjective process. The general rule we applied is that if a precast unit was chipped or cracked on arrival on site before it was positioned in place, it was replaced. A specified quantity of the precast concrete mix was to be retained by the precaster for replacing units broken or damaged in construction and for superficial repairs.

Stairwell and lift tower.

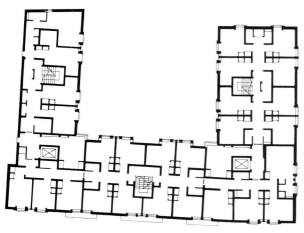

Ground floor.

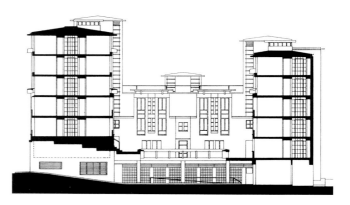

Section.

Basement level.

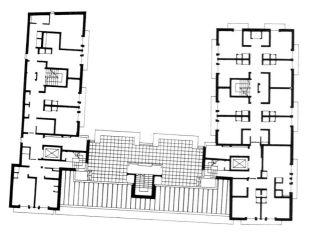

33

Cochrane Square, Glasgow
CZWG Architects

A handsome new city building in the heartland of Glasgow's commercial centre offers the onlooker and the city a new dynamic classicism, with a grandeur uncluttered by contextural mannerism, that is modern in style and composition without being too quirky, brutal or stark. Responding to the stone clad building legacy of Glasgow's merchant city, Cochrane Square's elevations and set backs of smooth, pink Clashach sandstone are contrasted by a series of three-storey high stone columns, the capitals of which protrude from the building line. The stone-clad columns are topped by giant column capitals which form balconies with an enclosing handrail, and takes the shape of a ship's prow, suggesting in a certain light that they could be a fleet literally sailing through the building. This touch of architectural fantasy and delight has put a smile and a grin on an otherwise monumental and stark urban fabric, giving the lucky commuters in this corner of Glasgow a moment to savour.

Cochrane Street elevation.

Location
The Cochrane Square development comprises one five-storey and one six-storey office block named Wheatley House and Cotton House, located in the commercial centre of Glasgow. The site is bounded on the north by Cochrane Street, by Montrose Street to the east and Ingram Street to the south. Wheatley House fronts both Cochrane Street and Ingram Street while Cotton House fronts onto Cochrane Street and Montrose Street.

Design
The site is on the northern edge of the merchant city where it meets the civic grandeur of the City Chambers building. The buildings in this locality are characterised by a mixture of period and architectural styles – for example two large Victorian sandstone buildings opposite the site – deploying different materials and façade embellishments. The majority of buildings in Ingram Street are of light sandstone and one of them is the grand Sheriffs Court immediately across the road to the south.

The scheme has been developed by HGB Properties in three phases as commercial office space, with the first phase named Wheatley House pre-sold to Glasgow City Council. Phase 2, later named Cotton House, was pre-let to the Inland Revenue, while Phase 3 has still to be built. Wheatley House is configured on an H formation plan, and the adjoining Cotton House configured on an L-shape plan. Both reinforced concrete framed buildings stand on a combined basement car park structure entered by a ramp from Ingram Street. The completed form of the development will be around a central courtyard crossed by public access routes via each of the adjoining streets. A secondary courtyard is formed at the west end of the development close to the party wall and car park ramp.

The elevations of the internal courtyard are faced with light cream bricks with bronzed window frames to reflect natural light into the courtyard. All windows on the south facing elevations are protected from direct sunlight by horizontal brise soleil. The street fronting external elevations are built of pinky Clashach sandstone blocks that have been quarried from the Inverness region.

The important façade on Cochrane Street has been designed to echo the monumental form of the Merchant

Precast yard and column capitals.

Outer yoke section of precast mould.

City Building and modelled with elements that provide it with a certain grandeur. Seven four-storey high openings with deeply recessed bronze window screens are bisected horizontally above ground floor level by rusticated stone beams on which stand lofty circular columns. The column capitals project forward from the plane of the façade to become balconies as they climb above the soffit of the recessed windows. These column capitals of precast concrete were surface finished to closely match the varying and subtle shades of the pinkish Clashach sandstone. The precast capitals allude to the prows of ships, celebrating the great history of ship building of Glasgow and the Clyde.

The stone façade between the tall window recesses can also be read as another order of pilaster columns supporting the entablature of the fourth floor, topped by a continuous recessed cornice. The cornice is a precast concrete structure faced with slithers of sandstone blocks. With the exception of the column capitals, the whole façade is kept flush along the building line and makes reference to 19th century Glasgow architect Alexander "Greek" Thomson.

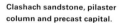

Clashach sandstone, pilaster column and precast capital.

On Montrose Street the façade is very nearly symmetrical and its more deeply modelled elevation expresses its unusual position on the Glasgow grid and provides a sense of termination of the building. Additional fifth and sixth floor set backs occur behind the cornice parapet which return to ground level and form recessed corners to the building. Functionally this also allows for the curve of the proposed tram rail in the street to turn the corner of the building more easily.

Construction

Architect's Comments: The precast concrete specification was based on standard clauses taken from the NBS specification on precast concrete cladding. A further note was added requiring the mould liner to be made from GRP or a similar material to give a finish to match the ashlar sandstone. When the first precast capital was completed a site visit to the precast yard was made to approve it. The surface finish, texture and colour match was very good. At the time the architect was not made aware of how the precaster had achieved the finish. It was assumed to be an 'as struck' concrete finish. The precast capitals have been in service on the building for several years now and look as good and as natural as the ashlar sandstone they abut. A small lead gutter positioned around the base of the precast capital was de-

Montrose Street corner and building set backs.

signed to trap any lime that washed off the precast units when it rained, preventing it from staining the stonework below.

Clashach sandstone was chosen specifically for its figuring, unlike most sandstones used on buildings in the region which were plain and uniform in colour. The stone was cut into 100 mm thick 'random' lengths of 450, 300, 900 mm blocks on the recommendation of Stirling Stone to ensure that it retained its natural stone character rather than give the façade the suspicion it could be facing blockwork. The precast capitals were left with a smooth unbroken stone face finish, to suggest that it could have been cut from one giant lump of Clashach. However, the recessed face of the large precast cornice was lined with random lengths of 50mm thick ashlar. Dark Brazilian granite was used at pavement level to mask the build up of any dirt staining.

Design sketches of capital.

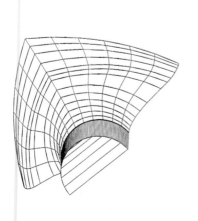
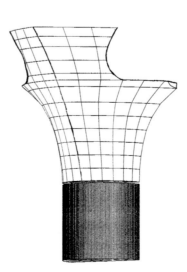
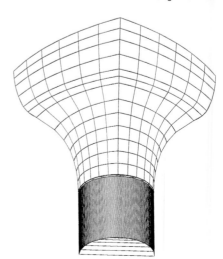

Four-storey high opening with recessed, bronze window screen.

Working drawing of column capital connection.

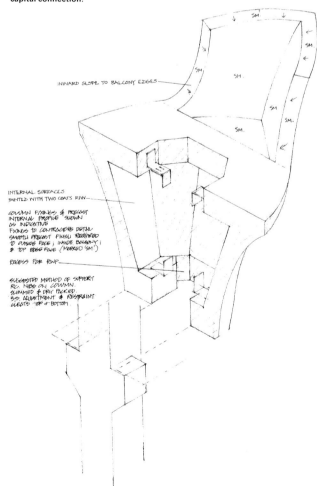

Client: HBG Properties
Architect: CZWG – Campbell Zogolovitch Wilkinson Gough
Services and Structural Engineer: Blyth & Blyth Associates
QS: Tozer Capita
Main Contractor: HBG Construction
Stonework: Stirling Stone
Precast: Stirling Precast
Wheatley House: 5 floors, gross floor area 5,135 m², basement car park, space for 29 cars
Cotton House: 6 floors, gross floor area 4,830 m², basement car park, space for 25 cars

Cotton House
Project Value: £ 7 million
Construction Phase: 54 weeks
Completion: 1996

Precast Contractor: Only one timber precast mould was made to form all the balcony capitals. The contact faces of the mould was fabricated from a lattice of timber lath which was in-filled with a stucco plaster and rubbed very smooth and coated with polyurethane varnish to give it an impermeable, dense surface. The lath and plaster panels were supported by a timber grillage of horizontal walings and vertical soldier supports. The complex conical shape of the capital was fabricated in sections, with an inner yoke and two outer sections that are all bolted together. Reinforcement was positioned around the central yoke, before the outer panels were positioned and bolted together. The complex shape of the capital was described in sketches and models prepared by the architect. Draftsmen at Stirling Stone prepared a number of working drawings to enable the joiners in the precast yard to build the mould. The mould was fabricated upside down with the base section left open at the top to allow concrete to funnel into the 150 mm wall void created by the 'stucco' faced panels.

The shape of the mould meant that internal poker vibration was impractical, so external vibration was used. As there was the risk of trapped air pockets and a large number of blow holes forming on the exposed surface due to the slope of the walls, the precaster chose to apply a thin render 'finishing' coat to mask the imperfections, rather than work the 'as struck' surface. The thin render coat was bonded to the exposed concrete surface once the blow holes were filled in and the surface was rubbed smooth. The thin 'finishing' coat comprised a mixture of selected sands and a bonding agent, which was blended to closely match the colour and texture of the Clashach sandstone. It had to be a thin coat otherwise the crisp corners, and tight geometry of the precast capital could be out of tolerance with the concrete frame and facing stonework that it had to dovetail. The concrete mix for the precast units was based on a white cement, a granite aggregate and selected sands to match the Clashach sandstone colour as specified by the architect. Had the method of precasting produced a blemish free 'as struck' surface, then the finishing coat would not have been required.

American Air Museum, Duxford

Ove Arup with
Foster & Partners

The design of the building brings the visitor into the enclosure opposite the immense glazed wall, leading to an elevated viewing ramp that runs down both sides of the building. Natural light enters the building from a daylight slot along the shell roof perimeter to illuminate the ceiling and the viewing ramp and to cast evocative shadows of the suspended aircraft on the wall. In winter months and during the evening an artificial lighting system is switched on to create the right setting for the museum exhibits. By day, the large glass wall on the front elevation appears almost opaque from the outside looking in. By night it is transparent and incandescent, revealing its priceless cargo.

Torus geometry.

Location

The American Air Museum is located in a hangar on the western end of the Imperial Air Museum complex at Duxford, 8 km west of Cambridge. Duxford has been associated with American military aviation since World War I and was used by the 8th and 9th fighter brigades of the USAAF during the Second World War. It was acquired by the Imperial Air Museum in 1972 to house the country's finest collection of British and American military aircraft.

Design

Engineer's Comment: For many years the Museum's collection of American aircraft – the finest outside the USA – had languished in the open air, slowly deteriorating and in constant need of repair. A campaign to raise money to build a giant enclosure for the collection took off in 1995, on both sides of the Atlantic. Hollywood stars Charlton Heston and the late James Stewart led the campaign on the American side, with Field Marshall Lord Bramhall leading it in Britain. With a grant of £ 6.5 m from the Heritage Lottery Fund, $ 1 m from Saudi Arabia and 60,000 individual donations from the fundraising campaign, £ 11 m was collected.

The overall size of the enclosure was determined by the desire to house all 32 aircraft under one roof including the colossal B52 'Strato Fortress' that is 16 m high and has a 61 m wing span. Some of the lighter aircraft, among them the famous U2 spy plane, were designed to be suspended from the ceiling of the structure, whilst the larger and heavier exhibits would be slotted around the B52 on the ground. The shell structure that evolved measured 90 m wide by 100 m long and appears to be partly sunk into the ground. It has an elliptical footprint of some 6,000 m^2 that recalls the profile of an aircraft's nose cone. The shell roof structure is highest at the front of the building where it behaves as an arch with a clear span of 90 m. The roof plan reduces in width and height curving inwards and downwards, becoming very flat as it reaches the back of the enclosure. The roof is constructed from two layers of interconnecting precast concrete shells. Each shell is 100 mm thick and spaced 900 mm apart. The membrane action of the roof allows load sharing in two directions, especially under the weight of the suspended aircraft. Forces from the roof shells are collected by an insitu concrete ring beam near the ground and then passed across a daylight slot via 34 steel arms spaced at 4 m intervals that are fixed to a lower concrete ring beam. Thrusts from the roof are resisted by abutment and spread foundations that have been excavated into the chalk ground.

Interior view.

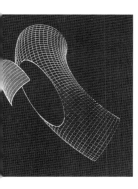

Shell roof enclosure and
mounded earth bank.

The choice of a double skin concrete shell was made
because it has good passive temperature damping, good
condensation control and provided an elegant and
graceful structure with a very calm background surface.
Early in the design process the team made comparisons
between steel and concrete roof solutions to show that a
concrete shell would keep the temperature above dew
point, eliminating condensation inside the building and
requiring only the minimum of dehumidification. Even
though a concrete structure was more expensive than
the steel alternative, because of its greater dead load and
hence the need for larger foundation supports, it per-
formed better on life cycle costing.

Completion of roof prior to removing falsework.

The structural behaviour of the shell roof was analysed. The analysis allowed for roof shell deflection, the effect of setting out temperature changes and even foundation movement. Lengthy analysis of the Duxford roof proved that the shell structure could be reinforced simply with just two layers of mesh of 8 mm bars at 150 mm centres. The 19 mm thick glazed wall panels on the front elevation rise to a height of 18 m in the middle. The glass panels are supported on a series of double steel mullions at 3 m intervals along the 90 m long elevation. The mullions are curved on the inside face and run from the roof to the floor – the taller ones near the middle of the opening have deeper curvatures than the shorter ones

Night incandescent.

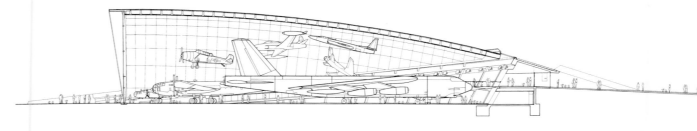
Longitudinal section.

nearer the two ends. To ensure the overall stability of the entire façade, the mullions are linked horizontally by vierendeel frames.

Construction
Construction Engineering: The geometry of the roof structure had to be designed in such a way that it could be easy to manufacture and simple to assemble. Under its own weight, an arch geometry would give an easy method of calculating the direct stresses in the shell but with a double curvature and changing radii such a shape would require a large number of unique precast panels to be made and fit together, like pieces in a giant jigsaw

puzzle. Because the roof has also to support point loads from the suspended aircraft and other asymmetrical loads which induce flexural stresses, it requires a greater section depth. This was achieved with the double shell arrangement which resolves the flexural stresses into push-pull forces that are resisted by the inner and outer shell. To solve the geometry problem, the shell roof was designed as a segment cut from a torus or doughnut ring, which is defined by just two curvatures of constant radius. In this way the precast panels could be manufactured from only six sets of formwork. To link the two curved shells, the lower precast panels have been designed as inverted T-sections which form ribs to stitch the upper panels to. The main structural function of the ribs is to resist shear forces. The lower precast units are provided with two steel sockets – with a carrying capacity of 13.5 tonnes – for suspending aircraft exhibits.

During the erection stage the precast panels were positioned along the crown of the shell in the middle of the span and working out towards the edges to accurately maintain a shadow gap of 30 mm between panels, for aesthetic purposes. The quality of the precast units were not up to standard when the first panels were delivered to site. We had to insist on better quality control procedures at the precast yard and for the installation of heating plant and protection measures during the winter months to ensure the concrete was adequately mature before the units were lifted out of the moulds and sent to site.

The glass façade was designed so that the components could be assembled on site, once all the aircraft were positioned under the shell roof. The curved steel mullions were erected on their pinned jointed feet and attached to the underside of the shell roof via a sliding joint. The stability of the mullion in the plane of the glass is provided by vierendeel frames. The whole façade can be lowered to the ground in the same way that it was erected to allow major changes to be made to the exhibition. This is planned to happen every ten years.

Perspective.

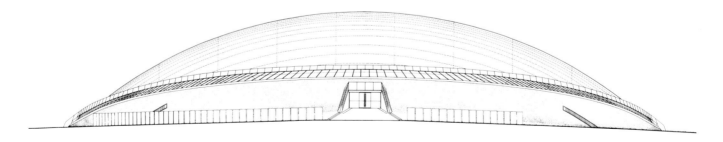

Rear elevation and main entrance.

Precast Production: The inner or lower slab was formed with the inverted T-beam, whilst the upper slab consisted of many individual 3 m by 2 m panels which spanned between the rib beams. The slab panels had to have reinforcing bars on all four sides to structurally tie the slab to the central support rib and the adjacent slab; this enabled the structure to behave monolithically. The inverted T-beam and lower concrete slabs were cast in sections that were 10 m long and 2 m wide and weighing 10 tonnes. They also had continuity reinforcement protruding from all sides including the rib beam. Whilst the geometry of the formwork panels was complicated by the torus curvature, the most difficult technical detail

41

proved to be developing a suitable insitu stitch between adjacent panels.

The solution adopted was to reduce the thickness of the inner skin from 100 mm to 45 mm for a 230 mm wide strip on the perimeter. This would enable a 55 mm deep in situ stitch to be made to connect all 250 projecting links. Slots had be cut into the moulds to allow the projecting links to pass through them and this made precast fabrication of each panel quite a challenge. The six principle formwork moulds were made of steel. Each of the inverted T-beam moulds consisted of a bottom tray curved in two directions and mounted on a rigid undercarriage designed to take high frequency external vibrators. The beam forms and rebated slabs panel edges were interconnected as one piece to enable the unit to be stripped and re-assembled in one single operation.

The original specification called for white concrete with limestone aggregates, but due to budget restraints a conventional grey OPC mix was adopted. To achieve the best possible surface finish and higher early strength for releasing the moulds, a superplasticiser was incorporated into the concrete mix. The reinforcement was assembled in purpose made jigs to ensure that all the projecting links were accurately spaced apart to fit the holes cut in the steel forms. Once each unit was removed from the casting mould, the projecting links were treated with steel primer to prevent rust staining the finished surfaces during storage and construction. The beam and panel units were lifted onto falsework on site and carefully positioned to maintain parallel joints and the overall roof geometry. When this was completed for all 972 panels, the joints were stitched with in situ concrete to produce a monolithic roof structure with a 90 m span.

Inclined columns and steel arms through perimeter light slot.

Abutment and lower T-shape precast unit in place.

T-shape precast unit.

Abutment and foundations.

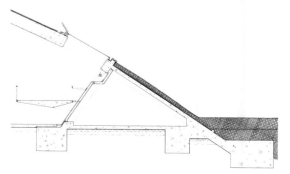

42

19 mm thick glass wall panels on the front elevation.

Client: The Imperial War Museum, Duxford
Engineer: Ove Arup and Partners
Architect: Foster and Partners
Services Engineer: Roger Preston and Partners
Main Contractor: John Sisk
Concrete Contractor: O'Rourke
Precast Roof: Malling Precast
Project Value: £ 11 million
Construction Phase (Structure): 12 months
Completion: 1996

Shell roof showing upper and lower precast slab.

43

River and Rowing Museum, Henley

David Chipperfield

Site plan.

The insitu concrete frame of the two buildings is supported on a series of pile foundations that rise above the river meadow like stilts, to maintain the ground floor slab above the flood plain. A wall of glass from floor to ceiling encloses the ground floor façade. It contains the entrance, the cafes, the administrative offices, shop, function rooms, toilets, library, lift lobby and staircases that lead to the gallery and exhibits on the first floor. In complete contrast, the first floor façade is enclosed by green oak timber cladding.

Location

The River and Rowing Museum is located in Henley in a river meadow and flood plain of the River Thames. The museum contains examples of rowing boats, racing shells and other river craft and charts the history of rowing and the River Thames itself.

Design

The historical sensitivity of the town, the famous Henley Regatta and the riverside location forced consideration of the external structure and language of the building as the starting point. The form of the two building blocks and the interlinking bridge makes reference to the work barns of Oxfordshire and the riverside boathouses at Henley. By adopting the pitched roof for the building to allude to these indigenous building forms, it was possible to explore more abstract and innovative treatment of the façade and structural finishes. It was also clear that any unconventional proposal that departed from a comprehensible and identifiable architecture had to be tempered by restraint. The design strategy was therefore to find a balance between pragmatism and inventiveness, convention and originality.

The site was formerly an overflow car park for visitors to the Henley Regatta, when it was donated to the museum trustees. The museum building had to be long and rectangular because this is the best ergonomic shape to fit the profile of a rowing boat. With a tight budget to work with there was minimal provision for landscaping apart from reinstating the reed beds and marsh meadow after the museum structure, the link bridge and visitor car park was built. The buildings were placed prominently on the riverside of the site to hide the car park and the cars and to avoid the mistake of having to walk or drive through the car park to find the museum entrance. The roof was pitched to resemble the upturned hull of a boat, with the ridge tile alluding to its keel. The upper gallery space is lit by natural daylight filtering through linear roof lights, supplemented by halodide lighting designed especially for museums. The building is naturally ventilated on the ground floor and air conditioned in the museum space. An underfloor hot water pipe system laid in a screed topping to the ground floor and first floor slabs, heats the entire building.

Façade detail.

Construction

Architect's Comments (by Renato Benedetti): Concrete was chosen because we wanted the building to be a minimalist structure with a boat house feel to it. We did not want it to be a structure just for a museum space but an open plan building that was welcoming as well. The ground floor is transparent and inviting, with the circular concrete columns and soffit of the floor slab clearly visible. The museum on the first floor is devoid of windows

Green oak, glass and concrete.

Terrace.

Link bridge and gable of southern gallery.

except for the linear roof lights, to maximise on the walls and the spaces within the gallery for the exhibits. Also the ultra violet rays of natural light can harm fragile wood exhibits and print under prolonged exposure, so omitting the windows had a double benefit. Wood was used to clad the museum half of the building in keeping with the tradition of boathouse construction. We wished to avoid the use of creosote softwoods common to many contemporary wood structures and looked for materials that required no long-term maintenance. We had considered using seasoned English oak but the cost was prohibitive, so we opted for unseasoned oak, which is often referred to as 'green oak'. Green oak cladding of a 400-year-old timber barn in Oxfordshire is still in pristine condition, weathering had only penetrated 3 mm into the wood, reassuring us that the timber would be durable. Only the external face of the wood will become weathered over the years and turn to a silvery grey colour.

Concrete Notes (by Renato Benedetti): As the architect we prepared a specification for the concrete finish and stated that the accepted finish would be based on a sample of concrete that the contractor would cast for a mock up panel. It was important that the contractor felt confident in achieving the standard of finish at tender

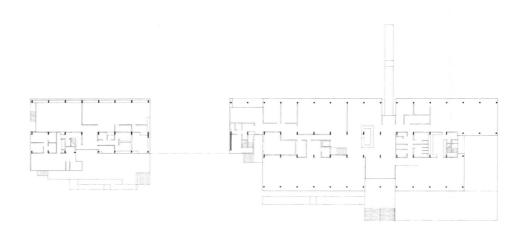

First floor.

Ground floor.

Car park (south) elevation.

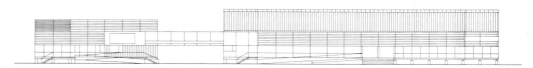

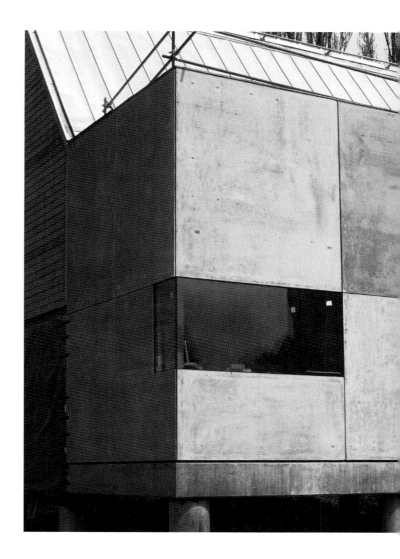

Interior surface textures.

Insitu façade wall and raised
pile foundation.

47

stage without loading the cost to cover the risk of rejection. We mentioned examples of good 'fair face' concrete to be seen on projects around London. We made a note of the specialist concrete contractor associated with those projects and insisted that Norwest Holst, the main contractor, employ one of them from the three names that we short-listed.

Generally the contractor used dense 'visaform' shutters for the walls and floor slab and metal forms for the circular columns. The 'visaform' produced a shiny finish to the concrete, which was acceptable, but the metal forms for the circular columns gave problems with the formation of blowholes. The reference finish for the

project was established from a section of a column face that had been cast for the mock up. Not all the concrete was acceptable, as there were far too many blowholes in excess of 15 mm in diameter in other areas on the same column. We advised the contractor that we could accept a few large blowholes of up to 15 mm if they were not very frequent; we were generally looking for surfaces with blowholes of less than 10 mm diameter. In the end the surface finish was a compromise between the contractor's reluctance to demolish any concrete and our insistence on the quality set by the reference sample. The contractor used the same pump mix for the casting of the columns and floor slab. The over-sanded pump mix contributed to the stickiness of the concrete which increased the risk of trapping blowholes against the metal formface of the column during compaction. A number of columns had to broken out before the metal forms produced an acceptable finish. The pump mix was adjusted to reduce the sand and to increase the large aggregate content to reduce the risk of large blowholes forming.

When it came to casting the exposed first floor slab soffit, there was a lot more discussion with the contractor to plan the pour, to agree the panel joint layout and the preparation of the joint edges to ensure no grout loss and to prevent workmen from walking on the shutters

Circular columns on ground floor.

with muddy boots once the surface was cleaned and the release agent was applied. The most difficult aspect was the positioning and setting of the box outs in the slab for the ceiling lights. In the end it worked out very well. There was no supplementary curing of the concrete slab, the columns or walls. Once the forms were removed the surface was left to air dry.

Entrance and staircase to museum galleries.

Steel work for pitched roof frame.

Construction of services corridor.

Architect: David Chipperfield
Project Architect:
Renato Benedetti.
Mr. Benedetti is now a
partner in his own practice
McDowell + Benedetti
Architects.
Structural Engineer:
Whitby & Bird
Services Engineer:
Furness Green & Partners
Main Contractor:
Norwest Holst
Project Value: £ 6 million
Construction Phase:
12 months
Completion: 1996

Memorial of the Synagogue, Wuppertal

Busmann + Haberer
with Zbyszek Oksiuta
and Volker Püschel

This is an adventurous and controversial building whose first impression suffers from the visual tardiness of a public car park and street market right in front of it. The garden of remembrance is overgrown and there are too many weeds growing through the granite paving slabs and gravel courtyard giving the impression of neglect. Once inside, the structure is bright and open to daylight illuminating the white rendered walls, marble floors and wood finishes. This remarkable cluster of small buildings cannot be appreciated from afar, because the horizon is dominated by a block of unfinished flats and a large department store. But within its confines, the shapes, the finishes and beauty of its sculptured forms dispel any lingering disappointment. The pale grey walls and pitched roof of the death camp hut in solid concrete is a counterpoint to the black lead cladding and redbrick façade of the other buildings. The huge disc of concrete pushed out of a skylight window is an intriguing yet puzzling structure. The ideas behind such visual oddities, when explained and understood, are both moving and enriching.

Location

On the spot where the old Synagogue in Wuppertal was destroyed during the Nazi reign, a memorial and a place of remembrance for the Jewish community in the town has been built. It can be found along Genügsamkeitsstrasse in the town centre of Wuppertal.

Design

The basis of the design centres around the indelible outline of the old synagogue in the ground marked by slabs of black granite. There is no simple way to reconstruct a building destroyed by the Nazis during the holocaust with stones and bricks to cover over the wounds. There is no architecture that can reduce remembrance to the level of a therapeutic matinee.

The new building is on a very sloping site with a large part of the meeting room and seminar rooms contained in a bunker like structure whose roof slab forms the courtyard, the formal terrace and walkway at the high end of the street. What is visible above roof level of the underground structure appears as a cluster of separate buildings, their individual forms and contrasting finishes of red brick, grey concrete, and black lead seem to distance them from one another. Yet they rise from the same base structure, creating spatial moods, and loose associations that try to symbolise the austerity of commemoration. The footprint of the old synagogue and the new building are clamped inextricably together. Their grids intersect and connect but are not congruent nor symmetrically disposed to one another. The black granite memorial slab of the old synagogue is visible on parts of

The site from upper Genügsamkeitsstrasse.

the main building floor. The massive concrete roof slab over the seminar room is pitched at an angle and rises above the elevated roof slab terrace like a giant disc of concrete to frame a curved widow. The bare unplastered exterior concrete walls and roof of the prison shaped dormitory block – a wooden hut petrified in concrete – where the day to day work of the centre is carried out, makes a powerful statement. The higher northern end of the site is bounded by a walled garden which is bisected by a stone pathway leading to the main hall. Next to this runs the archaeological remains of the boundary wall. At the lower end is a reconstructed façade from the time of the old synagogue and Germany's industrialisation.

Construction

Architect's Comments: The competition brief made clear that a monument for a destroyed synagogue was wanted and that the architect should collaborate with an artist. Our way of working was to create a living useable space not just a beautiful monument or a piece of sculpture. Remembrance is better reaffirmed by doing than by looking. A place to sit and talk, drink tea, listen to a lecture and hear a musical recital brings people together to share an experience. Perhaps in that way the youth of today can be engaged in learning about the past. So we suggested to add the seminar room and kitchen facilities to the brief.

Walled garden, stone rivulet and row of angled apple trees.

Zbyszek Oksiuta and myself spent the first four weeks just exploring our feelings, researching background material on the Synagogue, reading old Jewish newspapers of eye witness accounts of the atrocious deeds that were done to the Jewish people in the 1930s and during the war. Our first conclusion was to create a place where nobody should enter, a place that could not be made ugly. This was to be a garden based on ancient Jewish scriptures about white magic and the metaphysical 'secret' garden of purity. That was a cornerstone of our design. We thought of growing rows of apple trees at a deliberate angle in the garden, to parody the converging lines of a diagram drawn of the tenets about the secret garden in the ancient Jewish scriptures. We then built a pathway through the garden symbolising a watercourse, which is an essential part of a synagogue. It is a tradition that a synagogue can only be sited near a stream or over a well so that worshippers can be immersed and bathed at mitzvah ceremonies.

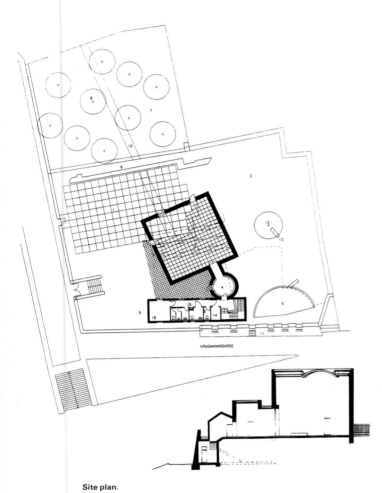

Concrete 'death camp'.

Detail of paving slab and
building edge.

Site plan.

Section through building
cluster.

Conceptual design sketch
of scheme.

Sketch of concrete hut
structure.

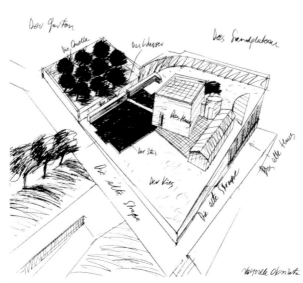

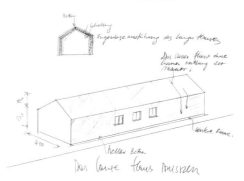

Concrete made brutal, raw and ugly.

Then our thoughts focused on how to work a plan of the new building spaces and to link the new structure with the ruins of the old synagogue. Rather than repair the walls of the old synagogue we left them as ruins and revealed the footprint that the old building once occupied, paving the enclosed area in black polished granite, like a large gravestone. A corner of the old building footprint passes over and becomes the floor of the new assembly building. The new buildings were arranged like large sculptures whose surface texture and colour are in harmony yet each one is different in appearance. We chose grey insitu concrete for the pitched roof as well as the walls of the stark 'concentration camp' building because concrete is a trivial material in our view and has no intrinsic character of its own unlike granite, limestone or marble. It takes on any form that you wish to give it. For this building we wanted the concrete to look brutal, raw and ugly. It will get stained and darkened when it rains and weathers. Once

inside the building you will not be able to distinguish one structure from another except when moving from one building to the next, as the interior finishes are unified. We wanted to precast the pitched roof but the contractor thought it best to cast it insitu on sloping falsework decking. The bare concrete has been treated with an anti-graffiti and anti-fungal protection.

The walls of the main assembly building are built of red bricks which look similar to the brickwork of the original building. One exterior face has been rendered and painted white to act as a screen for the single tree – a 'Japonica Safora' – planted on the terrace, whose small leaves rustle in the wind flickering their two-toned colours. The floor of the assembly building is laid with grey marble except where the black granite of the old building enters the space. The entrance rotunda is clad in black lead shingles, the colour of death, giving it a massive monolithic form. We wanted to maintain the same colour within the rotunda but the client preferred the white rendered surface of the meeting hall and seminar room. The steps leading down to the library and seminar room are diamond-polished concrete. The semi-circular concrete disc propping open the long arc of the seminar room window is reminiscent of the stone of a grinding mill that was found on the site. The large concrete disc cracked during placement but there is a

The 'sculptured' building cluster with concrete disc framing the window of meeting room below.

Assembly hall: black granite slabs mark the footprint of the old synagogue.

Client: Stadt Wuppertal
Architect:
Busmann + Haberer
with Zbyszek Oksiuta
and Volker Püschel
Engineer: Bonekämper
Project Value:
DM 5.5 million
Construction Phase:
24 months
Completion: 1994

base slab preventing any rainwater finding its way into the seminar room. The stucco finish and window details recreated along the sloping front to Genügsamkeits-strasse match the façade of the old synagogue. It serves as a reminder of the larger building that once occupied this site.

Meeting room and crescent window held open by the concrete 'mill stone'.

Residential Annexe, Constance

Christoph Mäckler

Coaxing a plot of land into a long, thin space for an extension in the most conservation-minded region in Germany needs the gift of a visionary. Bright, bold and full of contextual surprises, this ultra-modern three bedroom extension to a listed 16th century converted winery is in total equilibrium within its lakeland setting. Concrete is used as sculpture, as monumental stone that is bush-hammered, made smooth and cool, or hard and brutal in a solid jigsaw of contrasting style; shaping, framing and holding everything together. This extension could not have been built 100 years ago – modern concrete had not been invented.

Location

A private house on the shores of Lake Constance in the town of Constance on the border between Germany and Switzerland; it can be found off Alpsteinweg.

Design

A listed family home was to be expanded. The winery building had a strong presence of its own and was situated along the shore of Lake Constance. The design concept for the new wing was based on the idea to retain the listed building untouched, and not enter into a visual competition with it. The old building will continue to dominate the ensemble of buildings when viewed from the waterfront. Thus the new wing is not simply an extension alongside the old but makes it own statement in a very minimalist yet dramatic way. The annexe consists of two buildings of concrete; a long two-storey upper structure that hangs over a squat cuboid lower building. The white-washed walls of the slim upper storey structure houses three bedrooms and a lounge. The concrete walls of the bathroom cantilever from the white-washed walls and are left bare as beton brut, giving the impression of being detached from the upper block. At the front of the upper storey looking out across the lake, the solid walls are replaced by a glass façade framed by vertical steel sections that are punctuated by sturdy wooden framed windows. The lightness and transparency of the structure can be unsettling as the windows look heavier than the structure holding them in place. The client asked for a glass wall and a window to lean out of at the same time. This developed into brightly painted wood box frames with opening windows that are inserted into the glass wall. The upper storey is shored up at the one end by a single concrete column and at the other by steel bearings pinned to the roof of the lower concrete structure.

The lower part of the building stands half hidden within the sloping ground. It houses a vast room for entertaining and a small kitchenette. This half buried concrete

Kitchenette in the large basement room.

shelter is lit by two big concrete skylights shaped like wacky chimneys rising from the top of the roof. There is a glass panelled footbridge linking the old and the new building and a secondary entrance to the annexe which is independent of the main house.

Construction

Architect's Comments: There were two major requirements for the annexe that we had to address. One was to create a large open plan living space with a high ceiling for entertainment and family get-togethers and the other was to provide three additional bedrooms. They could not use the ground floor in the winery for this purpose

because the ceiling was too low – it was designed for the storage of wine casks and bottles. At times during autumn and early winter the permanency of the dense fog on the lake made the old house too inward looking due the low ceilings. We also had the problem of dealing with the local planning authority who were very conservative and reluctant to grant extension to a 16th century listed building. Nothing must alter the setting of the existing building along the shoreline, nor impose any changes to the landscape. Basically you can do nothing to a property in this region, unless it can be shown that the family have outgrown the accommodation. The client in the past four years had managed to have two sets of twins – from a one child family they had suddenly increased to five. The local planners were very sympathetic and supportive of our ideas once they were explained.

Of course there were planning constraints for the extension which we had to satisfy. We could only connect the

Shower room.

old building to the new via a particular end elevation window. Also the rear elevation of the existing house had to remain unchanged even though the façade had been restyled in the 1930s. So this defined the position and axis of the extension. It must be inconspicuous from the shoreline yet large enough to accommodate the space required by the client. We designed a long narrow building 5 m wide with the shoreline façade completely transparent. To further reduce the scale and visual impact of the building, the upper two-storey structure is detached from the lower ground floor structure and cantilevers out towards the lake, propped up by a single tapering column. The larger lower floor structure is set back from the upper floor and is partially buried below ground level and is square in plan. The lower structure is a cuboid with a floor area of 100 m^2, enclosed by concrete walls, a ground floor and flat roof; while the upper storey is only framed in concrete. It is clad in rendered brickwork along both side elevations and by glass curtain walling over the front elevation, and just a small pocket of 'beton brut' spilling out from one elevation for the shower room. The contrast and contradictions of material interplay create tensions in architecture – steel and wood, concrete and wood, warm and smooth, hard and cold. What we like about concrete is that you can express it in different ways – rough, close boarded, point tooled and smooth.

By partially burying the lower structure the impact of this large volume on the landscape is reduced. We wanted to give the concrete cube the look of a large rock and bush-hammered the concrete wall surfaces, except the deep reveals to the windows which were left smooth. After a few trials we concluded that tooling by hand without the aid of compressed air or electrical power tools produced the best results. Machine tooling produced a very rounded and synthetic surface texture, which we did not like. To avoid chipping the edges and corners a margin of 70 mm was created carefully by a combing tool beforehand. Although we were building to a tight budget there were aesthetic considerations which could justify the more expensive hand-finished approach. In years to come the concrete surface will age and weather and blend in with the landscape.

The metal formwork was used for the lower concrete structure which was coated with mould oil prior to concreting. A smooth, blemish free surface was not

Corner detail of basement
with bush-hammered
concrete surface.

Basement structure and
cylindrical 'chimney'
skylight.

Elevation showing how the
upper storey connects with
basement structure.

essential as the exposed aggregate finish would mask such variables nor was it essential to carefully align the tie-bolt holes. On hindsight it may have been better to have planned the panel layout and tie-bolt positions with the contractor as some joint lines can be seen, but it would have cost more to do it. Because the surface was to be bush-hammered, the plastic cones of the tie-bolt holes were left in place. To remove the cones and fill the holes with mortar would have made things worse in our opinion as it would draw attention to the fact that they were not aligned. The external concrete wall was insulated on the inside face, then brick-lined and rendered. The smooth, deep window reveals were formed using dense 'visaform' plywood. The upper storey shower room was finished with horizontal bands of board-marked concrete. The shower room cantilevers out from the floor slab creating a large light-filled space. The access from the lounge to the bedrooms passes through an open access at the end of the shower room.

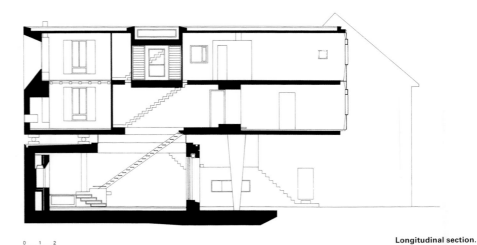

Longitudinal section.

Construction of insitu concrete basement walls.

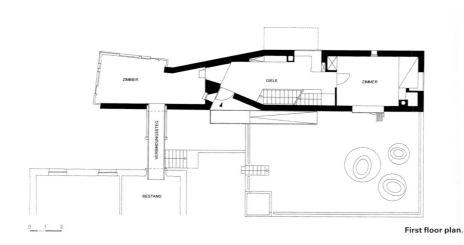

ZIMMER

DIELE

ZIMMER

VERBINDUNGSSTEG

BESTAND

0 1 2

First floor plan.

Client: Alexander Stiegler
Architect: Christoph Mäckler
Structural Engineer:
Bollinger & Grohmann
General Contractor:
Fischer GmbH & Co KG
Waterproof Concrete:
Zementol
Gross Floor Area: 288 m²
Lower Floor: 100 m²
Construction Phase:
12 months
Completion: 1995

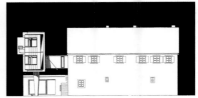

**Elevations from north-west
and south-west.**

The steel mullions framing the glass elevations were kept flat and thin to maximise the transparency of the storey-height glass wall. Strong primary colours – red, yellow and blue – add a splash of colour around the windows' edges, the walls of the external door and to the white-washed walls. The sail-like screens on the front elevation help to screen the glass from too much solar gain in the summer. The screens were made from sail cloth and the support poles and unfurling mechanism were devices borrowed from boat building.

End elevation from shoreline.

**Cantilevered glass walled
lounge and games room.**

Car Park Bantlinstrasse, Reutlingen

Michael Peter Architekten

Overhanging roof and mesh screen facing the road.

You have to rub your eyes again and again to work out the function of this sleek concrete structure. It won't be long before the telltale sign of cars running in and out of the building gives the game away. Seen from the back, looking towards the curved wall façade, Reutlingen's spectacular car park could be mistaken for a crisp modern office building with fancy external walkways, a grandstand building for a racecourse or the new wing of a school for the children of the wealthy classes. This is one of the most elegant car park structures built in Germany. What is so intriguing is that it did not cost a fortune;. it was well researched and imaginatively designed using simple and everyday construction details.

Location

Reutlingen is an industrial town in south-west Germany, just south of Stuttgart. The car park is to be found on the north-west outskirts of Reutlingen along Bantlinstrasse, one of the major highways leading to the industrial areas.

Design

The municipality of Reutlingen chose to commission a new car park on Bantlinstrasse following years of complaints from local residents about being disturbed by the shift workers of two large companies nearby, trying to find parking spaces. A design competition was announced by the municipality which would build the car park for 560 cars using public funds and the two companies would then rent all the car spaces from them. The site for the new park was on a triangular plot.

We won the competition because we were able to develop the site with an urban green space and to soften the visual impact of the car park structure on the residential area. We designed the building to act as a barrier to traffic noise and to minimise any glare from car headlights that could disturb residents at night. It has to be noted that when we won the competition we were not professionally qualified architects. We were working for

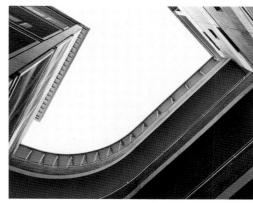

an established architect in town while completing our training and worked on the ideas for the competition from the bedroom of our parents' home.

The design of the car park was developed after studying the area and taking note of how traffic noise and car headlights could be reduced by orienting the car park structure in a particular way. The complex was split into two buildings, each with four levels of parking which were interlinked by connecting ramps. On the residential side the car park was curved in plan to follow the sweep of the two side roads. The façades facing the residential buildings were conceived as a solid curved wall of concrete five storeys high and 90 m long, with one storey below grade. The other car park structure fronting Bantlinstrasse was rectangular in plan with the back wall facing the residential area also a solid concrete wall five storeys high. The solid wall protects and shields the residents from traffic noise. Slotted openings were formed in the solid wall above the level of car headlights along each floor, to allow natural light into the building. The position of the window slots was made asymmetrical to avoid the stark and oppressive appearance of regimented rows of unglazed openings. In some ways the layout of the window slots was inspired by the punched computer card.

Internal ramp and slotted 'light' openings.

The curved wall elevation and access staircase overlooking the residential area.

The remaining elevations of each building are kept open but faced with a fine mesh screen framed by steel mullions. The mesh screens are an off the shelf item that is mass produced and comes in a variety of tinted colours and different mesh sizes. We chose green, copper, blue and silver tinted meshes for specific locations. The green and copper meshes for example are to be found on the external elevations facing Bantlinstrasse. The colour panels are randomly arranged to harmonise with the colours of the distant hills and brick buildings nearby and to make the structure appear longer. External horizontal louver panels fixed along each floor level contrive to emphasise the length of the building. The blue and silver screens are on the internal elevations between the two buildings. From within the building the screen is barely visible – the elevation above the car buffer rail appears open to the environment. From the outside and seen against the dark background of the wall, the coloured mesh is visible and tends to mask the

Invisibility of the screen looking out.

Roof top canopy.

Bantlinstrasse façade.

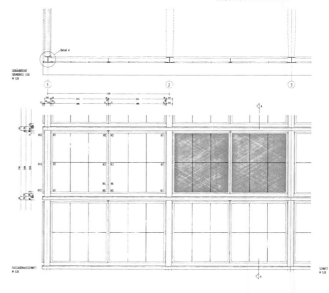

parked cars. Seen from an angle the mesh becomes opaque and merges into a solid wall of colour. We thought this would create a dynamic to the structure as cars went by.

Light is drawn into the building through the open screens, the window slots in the solid concrete walls and internal gaps between the concrete floor and solid wall. The composite concrete floor slab is supported on steel beams – at 5 to 6 m intervals – which span the width of the building to create a column free interior space 16.5 m deep. On the open elevation the beams are supported on steel columns, while on the solid concrete wall face they connect to encastre reinforced columns formed within the thickness of the 300 mm wall.

The smooth concrete façade on the residential side is broken by horizontal bands of external handrailing and balustrading of the access walkways – one for every floor. The walkways are interconnected by long raking staircases, reminiscent of the gangways of a passenger ship. The entry and exit ramps placed on the outside of the building was designed with a trapezoidal plate girder box beam with a curving alignment, stretching 16 m from one building to the next. It was fabricated to suit the slope and geometry of the ramp. One end of the box beam is fixed and the other is allowed to slide on a special bearing joint. The parapets of the curved ramps

Mesh screen detail.

and roadway sections were formed using precast concrete panels and insitu concrete. The more conventional internal ramps were built with steel beam supports and an insitu concrete deck.

A light-weight, profiled steel roof canopy overhangs the external walkways and is open down the middle section of the structure. It allows light and rain into the mid-section of the upper floor over the access roadway while protecting the parked cars on either side. The roadways lined on every floor are wide and generous as are the car spaces. There are no internal columns nor dark spots to hinder visibility within the car park. It is full of natural light.

Staircase.

Construction

Architect's Comments: The concrete structure of the car park gave us the opportunity to create a sound barrier and a clean monolithic construction with random slots for window openings. You could say it is a concrete canvas of abstract art. The openness of the structure meant that there was no need to provide a ventilation system to extract car fumes from within the building. Moreover as the building was not heated the insitu concrete façade wall did not require insulation nor protection against thermal bridging.

The control of the surface appearance of concrete was in accordance with guidance from BDZ – the German concrete advisory service – on visual concrete. The standard does not demand the best concrete appearance, but suggests how we may get the best from a standard concrete mix. We were trying to build a car park on a limited budget, not a cathedral. The concrete mix was chosen from a local supplier in Reutlingen and we selected a warm natural sand colour for the fine aggregate. In general we have been pleased with the standard of concrete finish to the walls, the floor slab and the precast panels to the ramps. Sure there were a few blemishes and discoloration to panels but there was no honeycombing nor grout loss. We have achieved 80% of the quality of a

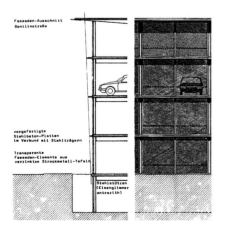

Sections.

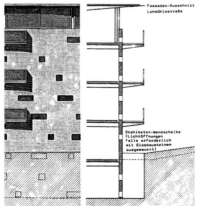

Curved screen wall with steel floor beams in place.

Blue and silver tinted screens on the internal façades.

cathedral-like finish to the concrete – typically one that Tadao Ando might have specified. To get perfection, the extra 20% improvement would have doubled the price of the construction and that was not sensible.

Construction joints, formwork panel layout and tie-bolt holes were agreed with the contractor in advance. The solid concrete walls with their window slots were cast first to their full height. They were poured in 2.85 m lifts which was the distance between floors slabs. Then the steelwork grillage of perimeter columns and principle support beams were erected floor by floor. Precast panels 100 mm thick were placed between the steel beams, the joints sealed before the rebar mesh was placed on the surface and a topping concrete of 50 mm was pumped into place. Once the concrete had been levelled and vibrated with a screed rail, the wet concrete was vacuum dewatered. This process is quite often used in Germany and it provides a durable, waterproof, hard wearing surface at an economic cost. The vacuum suction and mat filter were selected to ensure that only excess water in the mix was removed, not any of the cement particles. This process is effectively another form of vibration to the concrete where the reduced atmospheric pressure over a given patch of concrete draws out the excess water particles and consolidates the concrete further. It took nearly a day to vacuum dewater a pour area that was 40 m by 20 m. Within an hour after dewatering the surface was firm enough to walk on. Power trowels and power floats levelled and smoothed the concrete surface before it was covered with mats and kept moist for seven days to cure. When the concrete had dried out it was given a transparent sealer coat to ensure it was watertight. Thermoplastic road markings were applied to the surface for the car spaces and direction arrows.

A feature of the car park floors is the 150 mm light gap between the edge of the floor slab and the solid wall face which allows additional light into the car park. The edge of the slab is finished with a galvanised drain channel cast in with the floor topping, which prevents any run-off dripping onto the floor below. The light gap is broken at regular intervals, where the steel support beams ties in to the concrete wall. The soffit of the floor slabs are painted light grey to reflect light from the open elevations towards the back wall.

Client: City of Reutlingen
Architect:
Michael Peter, Markus Bauer
Structural Engineer:
Hans-R. Peter + Manfred Pluns
Main Contractor:
Adolf List GmbH
Project Value:
DM 14.85 million
Completion: 1993

Computer punch card layout of windows to shield wall.

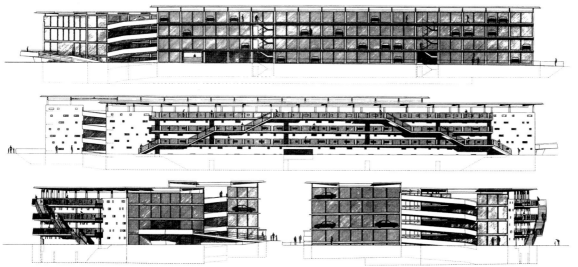

Elevation on Bantlinstrasse.

Elevation on residential side.

Lateral elevations.

Neanderthal Museum, Mettmann

Günter Zamp Kelp
with Julius Krauss
and Arno Brandlhuber

It is a shame that there is a bus stop and tacky sign advertising a tavern right in front of the walkway to this smooth, sinuous building. Built on a tight site in a clearing of trees, the windowless glass walls of this cleverly designed building hide the entrance from view until by chance you are right in front of it. It is a cave above ground, softly lit inside with walls and roofs of bare concrete which glows slate grey in bright light and remains dark marble in shadow. Down the middle of the spiralling concrete ramp, past the exhibits and displays of early man, a shaft of light floods the central staircase leading up to the roof, the balcony cafe and the sky. The museum is intimate and informative but it is the poise of this concrete monolith with its blue-green glass exterior that wins the day.

Central staircase.

Location
Not far north of Düsseldorf near the town of Mettmann in the Neander Valley is the Neanderthal Museum. It is along Talstrasse going north from Düsseldorf.

Design
140 years after his discovery, Neanderthal Man is getting a new home. Feldhofer Grotte where he was found was in a limestone quarry which had been extensively mined for many decades and which is by now just a landscaped valley. The exhibition building reflects upon the place of discovery and transports the original setting into a frugal yet powerful architecture. The new museum is not only a house for Neanderthal Man and his history, it is a reflection of the origins of modern homo sapiens. The exhibition is structured into a prologue and five episodes – life and survival, technology and knowledge, myth and religion, environment and nutrition, language and communication.

In the proposed design, by superimposing the idea of place with the uniqueness of the exhibited subject matter, the building itself creates an unmistakable scenario.

Its central theme is a spiral-shaped ramp which provides access to the different exhibition areas and defines the building character. The looping spiral access – a synonym for eternity – transforms the building into a spatial parable that unfolds the evolution of humankind.

The site for the new museum was on a flat piece of land, that was once occupied by an old stone building which functioned as a local restaurant. The form of the museum building is not in keeping with the existing architecture in the valley. Only the education section called the 'Pedagogicum', which forms one part of the complex, relates in scale to its local context. This section largely takes on the size and proportions of the original stone building. The dominant spiral shape of the main building can be read on the aquamarine translucent glass façade. An aluminium structure connects the glass panels to the perimeter concrete walls that enclose the building. There are no window openings in the cave-like quality of the interior except the skylights in the roof. The external detailing produces a striking contrast with the fair-faced concrete surfaces of the floor slab, the perimeter walls and central staircase inside. The spiral structure tries to give the impression of solid space winding itself out of the earth, towards the future of human existence.

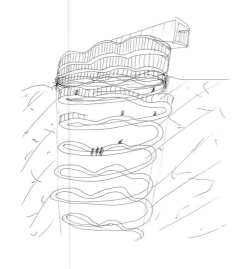

Concept sketch.

Construction

Architect's Comments: 136 German architectural practices submitted designs for the museum competition. There were ten invited entries from international architects. In some ways our design disregarded a number of the competition rules but this was necessary to preserve the integrity of our conceptual idea that the building form had to be spiral. The building was higher than stipulated to generate the required floor area within a footprint which we made smaller to reduce foundation costs. The structure rising out of the ground had to be formed in concrete to give us the freedom to create the plastic shape that we had designed. Concrete is a very adaptable material and has the flexibility to be moulded easily. It was also the most economic material for the structure but we confess that we had no practical experience of it before this project.

The concrete specification was drafted by the structural engineer and the contractor. We provided the guidelines and reference sample for the finished concrete. We referred the contractor to the concrete finish of the Harenberg building in Dortmund (Arch.: Eckhard Gerber, 1993–1994). In fact what was achieved on site was far better than what was expected and even better than our reference building. There were a few blemishes to the concrete surface but that was acceptable given how

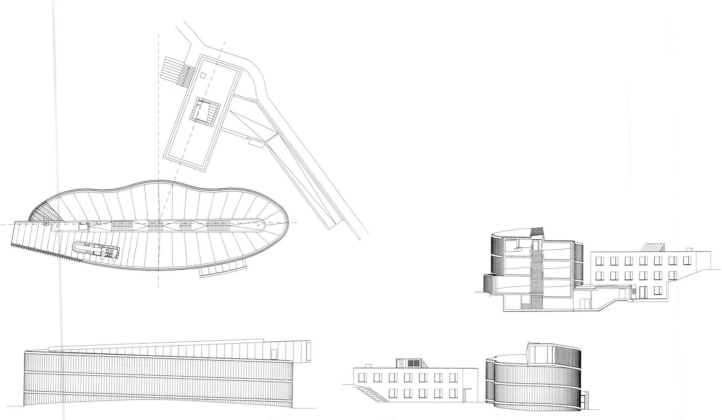

small these areas were. There was one patch that was honeycombed which was skilfully repaired to match the existing concrete.

Every formwork panel joint was mapped out on a CAD drawing. The curving line of the exterior walls was reflected in the curving panel joint lines that emerged and meant that there was very little re-use of formwork panels. It might have been cheaper to have maintained an orthogonal grid for the panels, but this would erase the flow of the panel geometry.

Contractor's Comment: We had to cut the floor panels to create oblique angled quadrilateral shapes to maintain the continuity of joint lines across the soffit of the floor slab. Consequently it proved difficult to get more than two uses from the panels. The construction was made more complicated as we had to integrate box-outs for the ceiling lights within the panels. The spirally rising, cantilever floor slabs are 250 mm deep and are sup-

Walls being poured.

ported on the 300 mm wide exterior walls that envelope the structure. Because of their large spans, two floors areas in the upper level of the museum were prestressed in the longitudinal direction at right angles to the cantilever reinforcement in order to limit deflection.

The fair-face side of the exterior walls – the inside face – was lined with wrought boarded douglas fir panels ranging in panel widths from 1.25 m to 3 m and lengths of up to 3.95 m and secretly nailed to a backing panel. The joint between panels was sealed with foam plastic strips. Rebar was positioned on the fair-face side before the other half was installed. Plastic spacers were used to maintain cover to the reinforcement and a standard

Glass clad concrete façade and window of 'infinity'.

chemical release agent trade name 'Lite Chemi' was used for debonding the panels after concreting. Walls were cast in 8 m long storey-high sections, with the concrete carefully skipped into place by a tremie chute in 500 mm layers and internally poker vibrated. The floor slabs were formed using multiplex emulsion coated

Falsework support for floor slab.

panels supported on quickstrip type falsework. Joints between panels were infilled with plastic filler and levelled out. The concrete was pumped into place, internally vibrated and then left with a tamped surface to key the 140 mm screed topping that followed.

A cement was specified for the concrete which was light grey in colour plus a fly ash filler. The total cementitious content for the walls was 390 kg/m^3 and 370 kg/m^3 for the floor slabs. The water-cement ratio was kept at 0.51 and water reducing admixture was incorporated to create a very workable concrete. The concrete in the walls were kept in the forms for three days in warm weather and five days in cooler periods. The immature concrete floor

South elevation.

Aerial view of site during construction.

Upstand walls on spiral floor.

North elevation.

slabs were kept humid under tarpaulin for three days. In cold weather they were covered with insulation mats. The walls were left untreated after the formwork panels were removed. Formwork panels were cleaned by brushing and washing after each use. Any damaged panels were removed and replaced.

There was one area of the slab soffit where the outline of rebar can be seen etched on the surface. It was caused by rust staining from the rebar during a very rainy period when the formwork was exposed to the weather while they were being fixed. This could have been avoided if galvanised or epoxy coated rebar had been used but the extra cost could not be justified.

A bonded screed was laid on the base concrete floor in two layers, without joints. The thicker base layer protects and surrounds the air-tight heating and cooling pipework for heating and cooling the building. The upper screed layer provides an 80 mm boring depth for anchoring the exhibition display units to the floor. The surface of the screed is coated with a hard wearing 2 mm epoxy resin pigmented grout and contains quartz to give the floor the concrete look. The heating system uses 14 brine-filled well points as heat sinks which were sunk 50 m to 70 m deep into the ground water. The system is reversed to act as a coolant in hot weather, for cooling the floors of the building. To meet the peak temperature needs ducted air is blown into the building via ventilation ports in the exterior walls.

The external face of the concrete wall is clad in double skin of sand blasted green tinted Reglit glass 50 mm thick, which is separated from the concrete wall by a 140 mm air gap and two layers of mineral wool insulation.

Client: Neanderthal Museum Trustees
Architect: Günter Zamp Kelp with Julius Krauss and Arno Brandlhuber
Structural Engineer: Bahlmann
Services Engineer: Pellege
General Contractor: Hochtief AG
Length: 51.98 m
Width (max): 19.00 m
Height (max): 13.59 m
Floor Area: 2,400 m²
Project Value: DM 12 million
Construction Phase: 12 months
Completion: 1995

Crematorium
Baumschulenweg, Berlin

Axel Schultes
and Charlotte Frank

You enter the tree-lined, gravel car park of the crematorium through the archway of an 18th century building with red roof tiles and white walls. You search for your landmark and notice its rectangular outline in the distance. The rectangular box gets larger and larger until climbing the front steps you are suddenly aware of the cavernous space within and a group of grey tubular columns soaring up to the roof. This monumental structure with its high walls and vast internal space is also surprisingly intimate once inside. Look closely and you will notice the wonder walls of Sakkara transfigured in concrete on both sides of the main hall. The blue tinted louvers of the huge glazed elevations bathe the structure in a bluish hue which gives the concrete surfaces a velvet sheen. You begin to speak in whispers not wanting to disturb the surrounding silence as you dare yourself to touch the hard, cold skin of these luminous cylinders just one more time.

Location

The crematorium is located on Baumschulenweg in Treptow in the south-eastern part of Berlin. It was the site of a former East German crematorium which it has now replaced.

Design

Unlike the towering mausoleums and monumental buildings of the ancient world – the pyramids of Giza and ziggurats of Ur and Sakkara which promised eternity and fulfilment in the afterlife – modern architecture can offer no such comfort for the dead, only a space for silent contemplation and private grief for the living. The dull, disconsolate air on the site of the old crematorium when we discovered it five years ago sent a shudder down the spine. A loveless aura warned the visitor: 'Abandon hope, all ye who enter here'. The heart of this architectural wilderness in our view needed replacing. Here where the dead will receive their final blessing with all the requisite sad routine, we must create the framework for a building structure that will respond to the ritual of the burial services, the provision of music and oration, and the feelings of the gathering mourners who need to pay their last farewells. At the centre of it must be a place which must weigh the ephemeral against the final, which amplifies the solemnity of such occasions and yet conveys hope and fulfilment in life itself.

In lending shape to the intensity and form of the new crematorium, the Maghreb mosque comes closest to meeting our ideals. It has a vast space in the centre where many can assemble and yet the individual is shielded somehow by the dominant central columns to provide a conduit for private feeling.

The crematorium's ceremonial halls for 250 people are simply large boxes of split stone, that are set open-fronted in a casing of glass at one end to let in the light, the heavens, the clouds and the trees. It is a hollowed, jointless block of concrete 50 m by 70 m, 10 m deep in the earth, 10 m high above it. Circular columns holding up the roof slab are spaced irregularly in the hall like a grove of trees, and are ringed by natural light at the capitals. Light is focused on a circular pool in the communal hall where water flows softly over the edges. There is an egg suspended undisturbed just above the water, symbolising new life. Natural light is controlled by large automatic movable louvers that filter and direct light to and away from the communal hall and side chapels. The building is a large stone, a grave-stone, the consistency of the earth itself. This architecture celebrates the sanctity of space and the silence of its walls bathed in light.

Construction

Architect's Comments: Initially it was difficult to achieve the finish to the concrete surfaces that we were looking for. While discussing the finishes we were told by the contractor's generalforeman about his concrete experience. What we heard made us very nervous and apprehensive about the quality of construction we might witness. He had spent many years working on the main sewer pipelines of Cairo, and on a prefabricated concrete box girder viaduct in Bangkok before coming to Berlin, but did not have direct experience of any fair-faced concrete structures and certainly nothing on the scale and ambition of the crematorium building. This problem was exacerbated by the inexperienced foreign workers often employed on German construction sites to avoid more expensive unionised skilled labour, in particular with publicly funded projects where there is a great deal of financial restraint.

So when the basement walls were cast it was not surprising to find that they were honeycombed and had grout

Front elevation and main entrance.

loss between the panel joints. Proper gasket seals between joints had to be insisted on and we even took the contractor to a builders' merchant to buy them. Sadly you can see some of these poor finishes at ground level along part of the podium wall near the entrance. Having resolved that problem, on the next pour in the basement we found that the concrete surface was dimpled with depressions like a mattress or quilt. The depressions emanated from each of the tie-bolt holes. It transpired that the tie-bolt holes had been over-tightened at those positions. A series of other minor mishaps followed which kept us on site far longer than we first planned. Once we had established the standard of workmanship that we had asked for and expected, we were able to reduce our site presence.

There were a number of items that we wished to include in the building which did not get built for financial reasons. For instance we wanted to colour the concrete blue in our original concept and that included all the walls. Using a cobalt pigment in the concrete mix is an extremely expensive way to achieve this, so we proposed that the concrete surface would be soaked and washed with a blue mineral stain after the concrete had been cast. The contractor was reluctant to do this for the simple reason that they had no experience with it; it would therefore be very expensive to carry out and that would mean sacrificing some architectural detail elsewhere which we did not want to do. In casting the columns and walls we insisted that no release agent should be used which could act as a barrier to the mineral stain penetrating the surface of the concrete. At that time the cost issue of mineral staining had not been raised by the contractor. Steel moulds were used to cast the 10 m high, 500 mm diameter columns. The inside faces were shot blasted and then lacquered to give a smooth, glassy finish which would make removal easier after casting the column. Formwork was left in place for three to four days and then the exposed concrete surface was covered with polythene for a further seven days. Unfortunately, by wrapping polythene tightly around the columns, we noticed this caused dark and light patches on the surface which we were initially trying to avoid. Ironically, we really liked the marbled effect this had on the concrete and were disappointed not to have tried the blue mineral stain on such a surface.

Grove of columns in the central hall and walls reminiscent of Sakkara.

Main chapel and blue louvers.

Columns heads ringed
by natural light openings
in roof slab.

Side elevation
and chimney stacks.

In general we like to detail sharp arisses and corners to the steps and edges of buildings. We had great difficulty persuading the contractor to form the horizontal bands of arisses that protrude from the surface of the 10 m high, 40 m long concrete end walls, like weather pointed mortar joints. Our original intention was to make the positive arris a narrow blade of concrete which would break to leave a fractured edge to give the wall a stone-like quality. Such a detail was first introduced in modern concrete architecture by Louis Kahn. The concrete colour and mix design was chosen from an archive of concrete cubes of various mix designs made by a consortium of contractors who work on Government and public funded projects. It was interesting to note that a cube made of the same mix three or four months later did not always match the earlier one for colour. Climatic changes, small changes in water-cement ratio, cement colour and ambient temperature can have quite an effect on the finished concrete colour. We chose a concrete which had a light grey cement – a ground-granulated blast furnace slag cement (GGBS) – with yellow sand and river dredged coarse aggregates. This produced a concrete which was ochre yellow not exactly the cool grey that we wanted, but it mellowed with time as it carbonated. The surfaces of the wall was rubbed down and water jetted to remove any minor surface blemishes. The 10 m high, 40 m long wall which was 400 mm thick was poured in three lifts without any vertical crack inducing joints. Sufficient reinforcement was positioned to control cracking and to limit the size of the crack width. There are no cracks visible on the wall surface three years after it was cast.

Client: Bezirksamt Treptow von Berlin
Architect: Axel Schultes, Charlotte Frank
Structural Engineer: GSE Saar Enseleit & Partner
Services Engineer: Brandi Ingenieure
General Contractor: Bilfinger + Berger
Total Floor Area: 9,339 m²
Project Value: DM 60 million
Construction Phase: 36 months
Completion: 1998

The concrete roof slab which has a large span, was cured for nearly four weeks before the scaffold was taken down. On removing the soffit panels the concrete was very dark and mottled in appearance. It was left to dry and carbonate for six months by which time it had toned down. Nonetheless the surface colour is darker than the column and end-wall concrete colour. However we liked the patchy marbled effect of the roof slab concrete once it mellowed, because it looked more like stone. When the cantilever roof slabs were cast over the entrance areas towards the end of the project, they were so light and even in colour – the forms and scaffolding had been removed after four days – that we did not like it because it looked just like a painted finish.

The floor of the main hall is paved in serpentine stone, not left as insitu concrete. We thought serpentine would take the wear and tear of foot traffic over the next 50 years much better than concrete.

**Entrance staircase
and cantilever roof slab.**

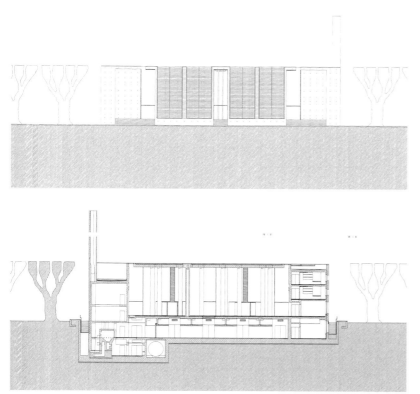

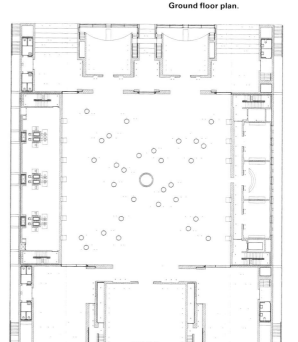

Front elevation.

Section.

Ground floor plan.

Arken Museum
of Modern Art, Ishøj
Søren Robert Lund

There is an immediacy about the long-angled white walls and steel-masted sails of Arken MOMA that beckons a closer look. The long blade walls of concrete, crisscrossing one another with surreal purpose and alluding to ships hulls marooned on a barren landscape, are intriguing and subconsciously uplifting because of their monolithic unity. Once inside the vast entrance vestibule with its feature spiral staircase and footbridge leading to a doorway going nowhere, the eye and mind are drawn to the tall, curving, light-filled corridors of grey concrete beyond. One easily moves through the meandering spacious halls to discover another space or corridor.

The external windows have been carefully slotted into position to provide a dramatic view of the wild landscape and sea, each one framed by the arms of those long blade walls. Architecture becomes art in Arken, and it is no bad thing if it provides an escape from any incomprehensible and self-indulgent artwork hanging on the wall. But when the art inside is just as good, we have double joy.

Sculpture courtyard.

Location
15 km from the centre of Copenhagen on the motorway to the south of the city, take the exit to Vallensbæk South, then find the beach road and turn at the sign for the museum.

Design
Central to the design of the museum has been the desire to create an interaction between the building and the existing coastal landscape with its beaches, harbours and lakes. In interpreting the character of the landscape,

Blade wall of art axis and main entrance.

the metaphor of the shipwreck has been very significant in the design of the building. By using this image, the design is inscribed into the history of the landscape. The metaphor is not treated as a formal element, but as a creative starting-point for the design. It is a story-telling element in the public experience of the building.

The museum building is centred around a long curved axis and embraces the surrounding landscape by extending three fingers of the building wall line. The outer foyer entrance is placed on the west side of the building and gives the visitor two choices on entering the building – either to move from the outer foyer into the 'Art Axis' space or into the main foyer. This creates a contrast between the intimate experience of moving from a narrow entrance space to the vast expanse of the surrounding landscape, the metaphor being a porch of a medieval church.

The outer foyer is situated between two curved walls – one from the art axis and the other from the main foyer. The steel structure of the roof canopy and the large steel gutter is placed as the intersection of these two walls, as a spine with ribs that stick out to penetrate the foyer. Rainwater picked in the deep steel gutter channel free falls into a manhole chamber, to create the sensation of gurgling water at the entrance to the building.

The main foyer is given its character by the presence of a domed-skylight, arched outer wall, and a massive boulder of Norwegian granite. An overhead steel footbridge, leading to the restaurant on the second floor, can be accessed by a spiral staircase in the main foyer. From the main foyer there is direct access to the darkly-lit ambience of the cinema and theatre room. The main gallery of the museum is the art axis with its length of

Opening leading into other galleries.

Craft gallery.

150 m. It is the unifying gallery in the museum. On one side the wall is crescent-shaped, on the other it is straight. The distance between them varies from 10 m at the central section, down to 3.5 m at each end. Notionally the space acts as the nave of a cathedral. From the art axis there is direct link to the other galleries. A wide, shallow descending staircase leads to the gallery for graphic art to the south and to the modular space and skylights of the gallery to the north. Others rooms and galleries can be accessed through large steel doorways along the straight length of wall.

The sloping, bisecting red axis corridor of the building, stretches from the main foyer and runs up to the res-

North elevation and sail-like roof canopy.

taurant. It is an important element in the architecture, making a visual connection with the interior and exterior structure of the building. The intimate character of this corridor space is emphasised by the tilting walls, the ruby-red colours, the floor-mounted spotlights, and the shiny, black floor. From here we proceed to the restaurant on the second floor. The restaurant is the zenith of the upward journey through the building.

From the deck of the restaurant the interaction of the long walls, the shipwreck metaphor and the link with the landscape and open sea can be experienced as one. The restaurant structure echoes the steel arrangement of the outer foyer, with a steel gutter spine and steel beams that stretch across the roof canopy like ribs.

Tilt up precast walls.

Art axis with curving wall.

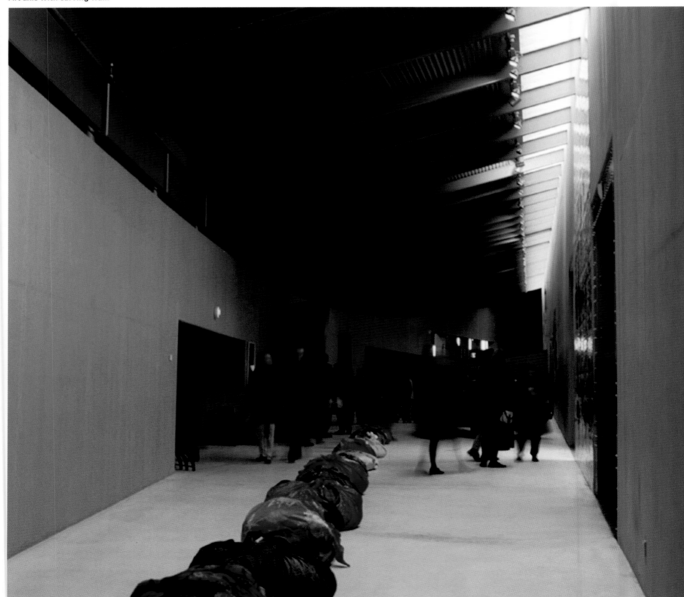

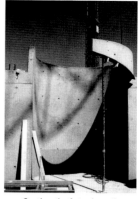

Casting the Art axis wall.

Steel rafter beams for gallery roof.

Construction

Architect's Comments: Throughout the design of the museum it has been very important that the materials and details are driven by the building layout and metaphorical connection with the character of the coastal landscape. In the original concept the building was designed to be marooned in the sea, with water lapping the seaward parts. When it was decided to move the building to dry land to reduce the foundation costs, we did not change the concept.

The Ishøj landscape is defined by its poetic wilderness. We have tried to use this character in the texture of the museum. As a consequence the main material employed is cast in place concrete and zinc coated steelwork for the roof canopy. These materials are carried through to the interior with white concrete floors, steel beams and steel doors.

The choice of concrete fell into place quite naturally when sketching and developing the shape and form of the building. Long thin walls extend beyond the enclosed space to create opaque screens that deliberately channel and define the views from within the building. The modelling of the monolithic walls to resemble a ship's hull came from studying images of ships in various books and after toying with a number of small paper models. The steel roof canopies on the other hand have been detailed to hint at the sails and mastheads of an imaginary boat. The nautical theme has been abstracted to the teak restaurant floor, porthole window openings, metal gangways and steel railings that feature along the corridor and gallery spaces.

A number of formwork panel systems were considered and we went on a study trip to Sweden and Germany to

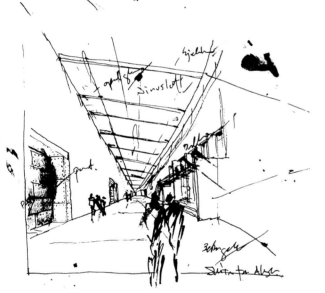

Sketch of art axis.

look at examples of concrete architecture to finalise the surface finish we wanted. For the straight lengths of wall grey precast tilt-up panels were used which were insulated on the external face then covered with block work and then rendered and painted white. The inside face, was skim coated and painted grey. The curved and angled walls were cast in place, grey concrete with the external face painted with concrete silicate paint, while the internal face was insulated and rendered.

We were on site quite regularly during construction, particularly when any new section of work was started, to check and confer with the contractor that the assembly was in order.

Contractor's Comments: In the basement we used a Peri formwork system with phenolic coated panels for the walls. For the exposed concrete walls above ground we used sealed birchwood ply with a spray applied release agent. The release agent was a water-based emulsion

Client: Arken Museum
of Modern Art
Architect: Søren Robert Lund
Structural Engineer: Carl Bro
Concrete Contractor:
Pihl & Son
Project Value:
DKr. 170 million
Ground Floor Area:
10,000 m²
Construction Phase:
24 months
Completion: 1996

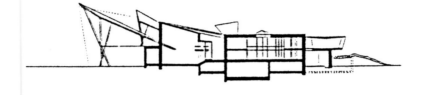

Sections.

Ground floor plan.

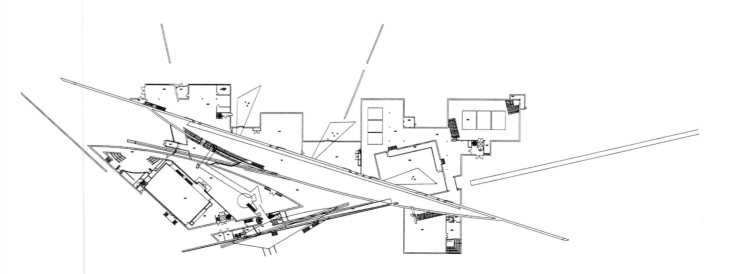

which does not wash off during rainy weather. Formwork was struck the following day after 18 hours in readiness for the next days work. The mix design strength for the concrete below ground was nominally 40N, with air-entrainment and a water-cement ratio of 0.45. For the walls above ground, the water-cement ratio was increased to 0.5. A water reducing admixture was added to improve the workability of the mix to give a 100 mm slump. Formwork panel layouts and tie-bolt hole positions were marked on drawings and issued to the architect for approval before concrete work commenced. We poured the external walls in three lifts – the maximum height was 6 m – and in lengths of 12 m. Concrete was placed by crane and skip and deposited into the formwork in 300 mm layers for compaction. For the 6 m high pour a tremie pipe 3 m long was attached to the skip to reduce the free fall distance and stop possible segregation of the fresh concrete in the formwork. As the walls were to be painted, we did not worry about some surface discoloration, so long as there was minimal honeycombing and only small blowholes.

A high frequency, internal vibrating poker with a 60 mm diameter was used for compacting the wall concrete. The 60 mm high frequency poker compacts effectively for distance of up to ten times the poker diameter. Achieving the quality of the concrete finish and uniformity of the panel joints was largely due to the experience of the concreting foreman and team we had on the project. There can be no substitute for good site skills and workmanship. However there is no recognised training for concreting operatives in Denmark, so we have to rely on them 'learning on the job' which is not very satisfactory.

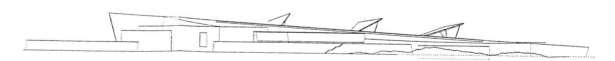

South façade.

Concept sketch.

Library and Culture Centre, Ledøje-Smørum

CUBO Arkitekter –
Peter Dalsgaard

From the outside it is an unprepossessing building, clad in black windowless panels, showing no warmth nor welcome. Once entering the building, the vast light-filled space that greets you is blinding. The repeating structure of the building is clearly visible and expressed very deliberately internally. The industrial grey concrete finish of the column and roof beam of the portal frames – blemished, blotchy and pitted though the surface may be – is surprisingly good to look at juxtaposed against the white-washed inner walls, the shiny steel finish of the profiled metal roof deck and the woody grain of the floor. The airy spaciousness of library and community hall created by high ceilings and an open structural form makes good architecture. The delight is in the clarity of execution and having the confidence to make economical 'unfussy' materials work well together. The black polished precast panels of the façade are perhaps an extravagance, because its real beauty can only be appreciated from a metre away when you can see the pearly grey slices of the granite aggregate petrified within the black marble matrix of the concrete.

Location

Smørum is 20 km west of Copenhagen, just off ring road 4. The Library and Culture Centre is along Flodvej.

Design

Ledøje-Smørum's new culture centre lies on a raised plateau in the urban landscape. The building appears as a long black box with a flat roof that is 72 m long, 15 m wide and 7.5 m high. The building mass is one storey high although it has three narrow, two-storey side wings that protrude from the north façade.

The black precast concrete façade elements are diamond polished to mirror the surrounding landscape and to appear as clearly described units. This is underscored by the large window areas which break up the monolithic exterior. A band of windows give emphasis to the top of the façade, while a long continuous plane of glass marks the ground floor on the south elevation and admits generous quantities of light into the building. Only in the foyer area, which separates the culture centre from the library, and on the north façade where the main entrance is located, are the windows allowed to rise to the full height of the building.

Rear elevation with footbridge and ornamental pond.

Main entrance.

From the central foyer there is an access to the cultural centre's main hall and the municipal library which occupies two thirds of the building. Access to the main building is through glass doors, which form part of the storey-high windows areas running along both façades. The lower part of the main hall has folding doors so that the foyer can be incorporated with the hall for large events.

The library is basically a repetition of the culture hall though it is more than twice as long. A book gallery runs along the entire length of one library wall and underscores the length and spaciousness of the room. Along the other wall, the partially inserted side wings

Libary and gallery floor.

are marked as two closed volumes connected by a short balcony. In the library the niches under the balcony are used as small reading alcoves and are equipped with low mahogany benches alongside the façade.

Construction

Architect's Comments: We won the competition for the culture centre because we made the interior very open, friendly and flexible – so we were told by the judges. The building was long and rectangular in plan with the long elevation parallel to the main road and set back some distance from it. This helped to reduce traffic noise and allowed cyclists and cars to access the centre via a slip road leading to the car park situated in front of the building.

The concept for the building was to concentrate the administration offices, meeting rooms and plant rooms into service blocks that protrude from the building line and are located on the wings. This allowed the interior to be one large clear space. The sense of spaciousness and light was improved by the high ceiling of the library, foyer and community hall. A building with such a large volume could be built within the fixed budget by using standard, factory-made concrete units for the frame and profiled metal decking for the flat roof.

Corner detail.

The deep precast beams and columns sections were assembled on site to form a series of portal frames. These are braced longitudinally by floor standing precast external wall panels. The proportions of the building were based on classical order, with a symmetrical rhythm to the window openings and external wall panels. It was important that the architecture was identifiable as a public space and not mistaken for a factory, supermarket or any other building common to the area. Scale and height were as important as the choice of a sober black concrete for the external panels. There should be no reference to red tiles which cover many of the roofs of residential buildings in Denmark. Black as a colour is fashionable and provides a sharp contrast with other materials.

Concrete portal frames.

On the front elevation the protruding blocks form an enclosed black wall line, whose continuity is broken by recesses leading to the glass-walled main and library entrance. The rear elevation overlooking the terraced landscape and artificial pond is one long façade with an unbroken line. Here the ground floor windows bring the parkland views into the building, and light to the reading spaces arranged along the glass wall.

In our original concept we made the exterior panels painted black wood but this was changed to black concrete following discussion with the client. A reference sample of black polished concrete was made by a precast company in Jutland to assist the contractor's tendering for the building work. Black concrete was produced by adding black iron oxide pigment at 6% of the cement content of the mix. Portland cement was used, and crushed grey granite imported from Italy was specified for the coarse aggregates. A description of the concrete and the finishes required was given to the contractor in the tender document. The black precast composite panels were later coated with an anti-graffiti paint.

The office blocks had all the precast load-bearing walls painted white. The landscape architect working with us laid out the tree-lined avenues of the front car park, the bollards, pathways and hardstanding near to the building.

Window and fascia detail.

Storey-high glass windows on ground floor rear elevation.

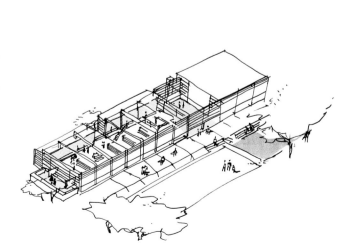

Sketch of building arrangement.

Contractor's Comments: The design information provided by the architect was quite comprehensive. We suffered from early teething problems in achieving the black concrete to match the reference sample. Unfortunately the detailed mix of the sample was not given by the precaster who made them, so it took until the twelfth sample panel to get a good match. The exterior composite precast panels comprised an inner load-bearing section 200 mm thick, then 100 mm of insulation and 80 mm of facing black concrete. The panels were cast in 6 m lengths and in two set heights, to suit the finished building line. The panels were cast in forms on the ground and poured in sequence finishing with the black concrete layer on the top. The load-bearing section was fully reinforced and tied to the mesh of the facing concrete through the insulation layer. The black concrete was trowelled to a smooth finish and then diamond-polished by wet grinding. Some panels were found to have too many blowholes and blemishes on the site after they had been erected. Rather than remove these panels and disrupt progress on the building work, we decided to erect a scaffold and hand grind all the panels insitu. It took over two months to complete.

Generally construction work went very well but there was one further problem which caused accidental staining and marking to the exposed concrete face of the por-

92

tal frames. When the roof was being installed the roofers were unaware that the concrete of the portal frames was the final finish, and thinking it was to be painted they allowed rainwater to run down and dabbed paint on the surface to mark datum levels. The entire surface of the beams and columns had to be cleaned and cement rendered to hide these marks. It would have been prudent for the architect to have mentioned this in the specification that was issued to the roofing contractor.

Site plan.

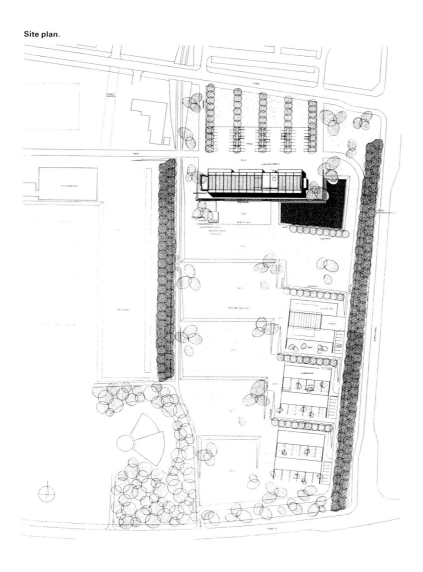

Client: City of Ledøje-
Smørum
Architect: CUBO Architekter -
Peter Dalsgaard
*Structural and Services
Engineer:* Dominia
Landscape Architect: Preben
Skaarup
Main Contractor: B. Nygaard
Sorensen
Project Value: DKr. 25 million
Construction Phase:
12 months
Completion: 1999

**Polished black concrete
panels.**

Minnaert Building, Utrecht University
Neutelings Riedijk

Unconventional and quirky in every detail, conceived by a wild imagination and the desire to be different and glitzy can be the reaction on seeing the building at first glance. Rarely can it be said of a building, built to such a tight budget and on such an industrial scale, that it takes the breath away for the sheer power of its architectural creativity. Fit for purpose, it has satisfied all the criteria and standards for comfort and accommodation and delivered far more – a healthy working environment, light-filled spaces and a stimulus for the senses. The structure offers many innovations for the discerning onlooker to admire. Factory-made standardised construction components have been skilfully engineered by Rob Nijsse, adding to the sculptural mastery of the architecture. And Neutelings'gift for delight and surprise is visible everywhere. The most vivid canvas is the exploitation of pigmented sprayed concrete for the exterior. For underground tunnels shotcrete is ok, but exposing it on a prestigious building is unheard of. The Minnaert Building stretches the boundaries of what is possible and practical with modern concrete and succeeds beyond expectation.

Location
The Minnaert Building is located in the campus of the University in Utrecht and is the central faculty building for the Beta Sciences.

Design
The Minnaert Building in one more step in the process of filling and linking up the existing network of the north-western corner of the University campus. The programme for the Minnaert Building comprises three main

South-west view.

elements: classrooms and laboratories, a restaurant serving the entire north-western corner of the campus and a workspace for three departments. These functional requirements are complemented by the 'tare space' – an undefined area made up of circulation and service zones. The basic idea was to concentrate as much tare space as possible in one large attractive hall on the first floor. It was to be the transit area and meeting place for everybody in this part of the campus.

The main feature of the central hall is a large 10 by 50 m pond that collects rainwater from the roof via large open channels in the roof space. This water basin is used for natural cooling of the building. During the day, it is pumped through the building to absorb the excess heat generated by people, computers, lighting and machines and in the evening the water is pumped back over the roof to be cooled by the night air. When it rains, the water falls noisily into the hall, raising the basin level and creating a tidal effect. The building roof structure consists of precast concrete panels suspended from deep girder beams which allows a large column-free space over the water basin. The external façade is coated with a thick layer of undulating gunite concrete infused with a terra cotta pigment. This treatment enhances the monolithic appearance of the building.

Part of the ground floor on the front elevation is an open bicycle park. A row of slender steel ground floor columns support the front edge of the building. Some of them are configured graphically to form the letters of the Belgian physicist after whom the building is named – Marcel G Minnaert had been a professor in astronomy at the University in the 1930s.

Sprayed coloured concrete façade and ripple contours.

94

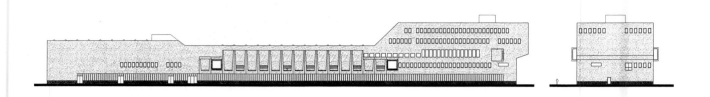

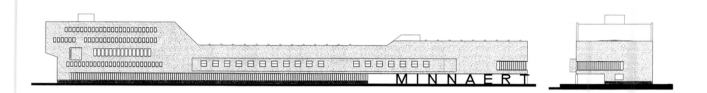

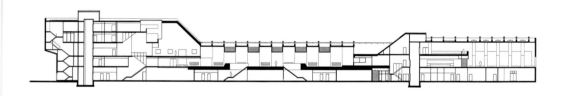

North elevation.

South elevation.

Longitudinal section.

Ripple detail at window openings.

Construction

Engineer's Comment (Rob Nijsse, ABT): The University
had set out a very detailed brief, with the exact space
requirement for the laboratories, the seminar room, the
staff rooms, desks, catering facility, the exits, doors,
toilets, etc. To comply with all these strictures it would
have been easiest to programme everything into
repeating rectangular boxes divided by three floors and
cover it with a roof. Half joking, the first idea was to
create a big excavation and construct the building below
the ground. But we concluded it would be more
interesting to have a visible building with the façade
irregular and red-brown in colour suggesting that the
building had been pushed out of the earth. This in fact is
what we have designed – a cave in the air. We wanted to
transform the central section of the first floor into a vast
column-free concourse and feature a pool of water filled
by rainwater collected from the roof. At the eastern end
of this long central section we positioned the large
communal dining room. We were able to zone and fit all
the laboratories for each department, plus the lecture
rooms on the ground floor and to contain the administrative offices in a multi-storey block attached to the
western end of the building. All these sections could be
accessed from the first floor concourse. The space
requirements met the brief in every respect. We kept the
cost of the construction within budget by adopting
standard prefabricated precast structural components to
frame and enclose the building.

The vast open floor area over the water pool is bridged
by 20 m long precast roof girder beams which are supported on vertical panel walls of sandwich construction,
stiffened with counterfort sections at the roof beam positions. Flat precast panels clamped to the underside of
the tapered concrete roof beams, form the roof canopy
over the water pool. The threaded bolts and brackets that
connect the panels to the beams and one another are
expressed on the soffit. The neat and orderly arrangement of these visible connections add to the rigour of the

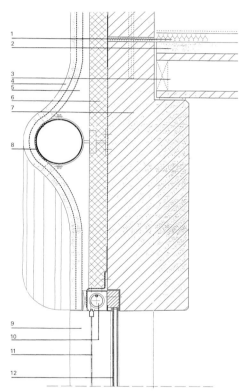

**Detail of external wall
construction.**

1	Floor finishing with tiles
2	Screed floor
3	Concrete hollow core floorslab
4	Shotcrete
5	Ventilated cavity wall
6	Insulation
7	Prefabricated concrete element
8	Vapour barrier
9	Steel mullions on fixeners with thermal break
10	Sun screen box
11	Sun screen
12	Insulated glass

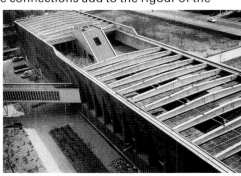

View from above.

Communal dining room.

architecture. The inside face of the inclined panels is lined with grey terrazzo tiles to give a smooth, stain free surface along the water line and protection from splashes of rainwater that cascade down the roof channels into the pool. Within the open concourse, adjacent to the pool, are rows of dining booths detailed to resemble a line of carriages each with a facing pair of red upholstered bench seats separated by an oblong dining table and with individual bay windows. They have been nicknamed the 'kissing rooms'. The booths cantilever out from the first floor to increase natural light penetration. Five rectangular concrete open channels collect the rainwater from the roof and direct it into the pool through roof openings. About 70% is used for flushing toilets and cleaning purposes to reduce the demand on potable water. The pool can store 200,000 litres of 'grey' water and also serves as a heat sink for heating and cooling the building. The first floor and upper administration floors are reinforced coffered slabs supported on circular columns. Having transformed the inner space of the building, we toyed with ideas on how to create the effect of an earth-like covering to the façade and proposed that it could be done using sprayed concrete with a brown-red pigment. We also had to place the name of the building on the structure that would be visible and obvious. Rather than putting it – as customary – on the roof we used the steel composite columns on the front elevation to create the letters. The letters were formed using 400 mm^2 hollow steel sections filled with 25N concrete and internally reinforced.

Sprayed Concrete Comments (Peter Nuiten, BIM): The architect wanted to replicate the ripples of sand on a beach at low tide onto the façade. As the specialist sprayed concrete (shotcrete) contractor we had a number of technical problems to overcome before we found a method that gave consistent results. First of all the plastic tubes that we used to create the ripple effect were not flexible enough to bend to the deflected shapes

First floor grey water pool
and kissing booths.

The letters in hollow steel
sections.

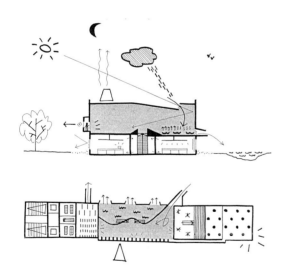

Diagram of natural cooling.

100 mm insulation panels
pinned to concrete wall.

Tying reinforcement mesh.

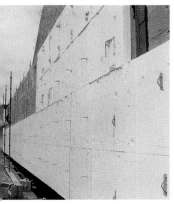

that the architect wanted, so the ripple contours were reduced in curvature. Our other concern was the need for a lot more construction joints on the façade to minimise the risk of random cracking of the 50 mm concrete skin and to ensure crack widths did not exceed 0.3 mm for water tightness. The joint positions were agreed and they were quite well concealed. After extensive trials to find the best way to bond the sprayed concrete to the 100 mm thick polystyrene insulation we tested a geotextile fabric backing, glass fibre cement boards – the best adhesion was found by spraying directly onto the insulation.

The Minnaert Building was the first building to use coloured shotcrete on such a scale, so there were some inevitable early problems. The concrete was brought ready mixed to the site by truck, and the pigment was added using a dosing pump in one cubic metre batches, before delivery to the gunite machine. The pigment colouring was too patchy and variable and after spraying

100 m² we abandoned this technique. The pigment batch quantity was too small and there were blockages occurring in the dosing pipes. To improve the colour consistency we decided to install a static 6 m³ drum mixer on site. The ready mix truck discharges its full load into the static mixer, the correct pigment dosage is added and then the concrete is mixed for 30 minutes for even colour. 6 m³ is enough to cover 100 m² of sprayed concrete allowing for rebound losses, and that represented a day's work for the crew.

The elevation was fully scaffolded and boarded before spraying progressed in horizontal bands from the bottom to the top of the structure. It was necessary to spray the concrete skin in two passes each of 25 mm depth. There was very little rebound losses against the polystyrene backing – it was nearer 20% against the inner layer of shotcrete. Because we had to work in 2 m high lifts that ran horizontally across the elevation, there were the inevitable tell-tale lines where the scaffold plank and the

Wet gunting pigmented
concrete.

continuity joint existed and where the spray pressure varied as the gun was angled to reach the very top and bottom of the lift. There was little we could do to eliminate this. Variation in pigment concentration showed between batches, exacerbated by climatic change during the construction period – darker in tone in cold and humid weather and lighter in hot and windy weather. Seen from 20 m away the façade is nearly homogeneous and gives the appearance of a deep-piled carpet, but at close quarters the aggregate texture and colour variation become very noticeable.

The cement content of the mix was 475 kg/m^3 and consisted of 60% OPC and 40% blast furnace slag cement. The water-cement ratio was kept to 0.41, helped by the addition of Rheobuild 2000 superplasticiser. The maximum aggregate size was 8 mm, the sand and gravel proportion was gauged in accordance with the Dutch shotcrete standard. Micro silica was added at 2% of cement content while retarder was added at 0.6% and an activator was introduced at 3% of cement mass. The concrete was retarded as a precaution against any blockages forming in the feed line to the nozzle. At the nozzle the mix was activated with a solution of Meyco SA145. The redbrown pigment was based on Bayferrox 110 having a solids content of 60% and dispensed at a dosage rate of 6% of cement content.

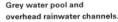
South elevation.

Three years on and the surface of the concrete is in pristine order – no lichen nor algae growth nor water stains or lime bloom are to be seen. That has come as a disappointment to the architect who had hoped to see the surface covered in patches of moss or lichen growth and weathered to give it the appearance of a large rock formation.

Client: University of Utrecht
Architect: Neutelings Riedijk/ Willem Jan Neutelings, Michiel Riedijk
Structural Engineer: ABT/Rob Nijsse
Services Engineer: Linssen bv
Landscape Architect: West 8
Main Contractor: JP van Eesteren
Sprayed Concrete: BIM
Length 150 m; width 22 m; height over central section 12.5 m; maximum height 22 m
Floor Area: ground 2,900 m^2; lst 3,300 m^2; 2nd 1,230 m^2; 3rd 1,000 m^2; 4th 950 m^2
Project Value: NLG 28 million
Construction Phase: 36 months
Completion: 1998

Grey water pool and overhead rainwater channels.

Study area, second
floor administration block,
overlooking pool.

Moebius House, Naarden

Ben van Berkel/UN Studio

'If we can make a model in cardboard we can build it in concrete', they say at Ben van Berkel/UN Studio. In this case, the ground floor is wrapped in a skin of glass that is sometimes clear and sometimes translucent depending on which part of the concrete structure is directly behind it. The house is conventional in function yet stands almost shapeless and organic in the landscape. It is private and intimate and very much part of the woodland setting rather than an entity remote from it. Sleeping, working and communal spaces flow from one to the other without obvious demarcation by doorways or thresholds. The client's collection of paintings are hung along the concrete corridor walls like in an art gallery – a corridor that leads to the upper and lower bedrooms and terrace spaces.

The vast, light-filled lounge, kitchen and dining room are loosely collected in one large space, partially separated by thick, not very long panels of concrete wall, often punctuated with clear slots at the base to appear as gravity defying screens. They also support the suspended floor slab and cantilever balconies above. The screen walls of light grey concrete transform into furniture near the base – they can be long narrow cantilever shelves or a chimney breast or dining table. The effect is stunning. In situ cast concrete, sprayed concrete, precast terrazzo concrete and glass and wood flooring are the materials chosen by the architect to create a building that has taken five years to realise.

Elevation detail.

Location

The Moebius House is situated along a private road in a leafy woodland setting 30 km from Amsterdam, between the villages of Naarden and Huizen.

Design

The diagram of the double-locked torus conveys the organisation of two intertwining paths, which trace how two people can live together, yet apart, meeting at certain points which then become shared spaces. The idea is extended to include the material of the building and its construction.

The Moebius House integrates programme, circulation and structure seamlessly. The house interweaves the various states that accompany the distillation of differentiating activities into one work structure: work, social and family life and individual time all find places in the loop format. The structure of this movement is transferred to the organisation of the two main materials used for constructing the house. Glass and concrete move in front of one another and switch places – concrete becomes furniture and glass turns into partition walls.

As a graphic representation of 24 hours of family life, the torus diagram acquires a time-space dimension which leads to the implementation of the Moebius band. Equally the site and its relationship to the building are important for the design. The site covers two hectares which is divided into four areas – the parallel road, the meadows, the hill and the woods – that are distinct in character. Linking these with the internal organisation of the Moebius band transforms living in the house into a walk in the landscape.

The mathematical model of the Moebius band is not literally transferred to the building, but is conceptualised and can be found in the architectural ingredients, such as

Transparency of architecture.

the light, the staircases and the circulation. So, while the Moebius diagram introduces aspects of event-duration and trajectory, it is worked into the building in a mutated way.

The instructiveness of this simple, borrowed form is the key in the design. The two interlocking lines are suggestive of the formal organisation of the building, but that is only the beginning; diagrammatic architecture such as this liberates architecture from stylised language, conventional interpretation and contextual mannerism.

Construction

Architect's Comments: From the survey of the site we wanted the new house to have the opposite orientation as an existing house. We preferred a north-south axis to minimise the number of trees we would have to remove and to harmonise the much larger footprint with the landscape. If you change the orientation of a house in a conservation area such as Naarden you have to go

North-west elevation.

through a lot more red tape. The proposed design and layout for the Moebius House had not only to satisfy the local planning authorities but it had to be approved by a so-called "beauty committee." This committee is made up of often elderly architects working in the region, and they have to ensure that any new building is not detrimental to the existing environment or character of the region. To explain our ideas we made models and developed three-dimensional CAD images to express the architecture. After some discussion and a number of consultations we were pleasantly surprised when planning consent was given unreservedly.

We prepared contract drawings showing all the principle details and finishes. There was a method statement which described how the concrete work had to be carried out and related to texture, colour and uniformity of surface finishes and dimensional accuracy. The contractor was required to produce a sample panel which when approved would set the standard for the rest of the work.

Wash basin and concrete interior.

Cantilever concrete dining table built into column.

It took almost a year to find a contractor who could do the work within the budget that the client had in mind. When the job was first tendered all four bids were way over the budget. Even when we tried negotiating with the lowest tenderer we had to abandon further discussion after a year, when it became apparent that the final price was still too high. Just when we thought the project would have to be shelved, the engineer suggested a local firm, Kemmeren Bouw, who had expressed an interest in the project. Kemmeren negotiated a price with us, and the client gave the go-ahead soon afterwards. Their price was 40% less than the lowest earlier tender figure.

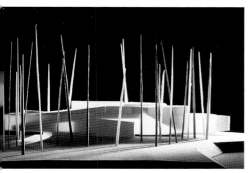

Modelling the building shape.

Glass wrapped over concrete creating an opaque screen.

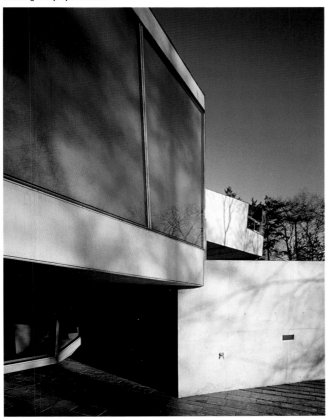

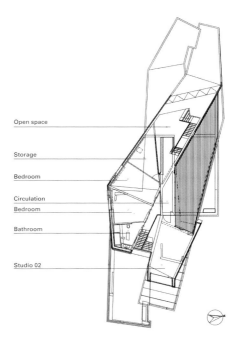

Open space

Storage

Bedroom

Circulation

Bedroom

Bathroom

Studio 02

Floor plan level 3.

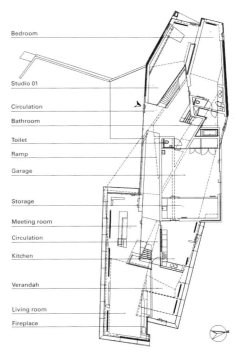

Bedroom

Studio 01

Circulation

Bathroom

Toilet

Ramp

Garage

Storage

Meeting room

Circulation

Kitchen

Verandah

Living room

Fireplace

Floor plan level 2.

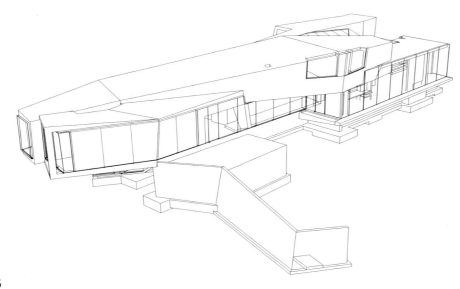

Axonometric view of north elevation.

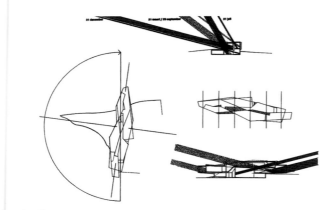

Location diagrams.

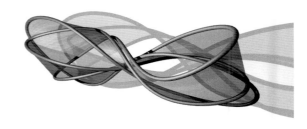

Projection of Moebius principle.

Contractor's Comments: This was not a conventional project. No two walls, edge beams or floor slabs were the same. Not only were walls built on a slope they were made deliberately out of plumb or sometimes suspended from the floor above to clear the lower floor by 300 mm. A solid concrete wall panel suspended from the roof could turn into a long cantilever slab to form the dining table. Every element of formwork was cut to very precise measurement like making fitted wardrobes. Formwork panels had to be aligned using survey instruments and accurate tape measurements to ensure that the top of the structure ended up in the right position. We had to make a series of large scale working drawings to show the carpenters on site just how to form the walls. More importantly we employed skilled men who could think three dimensionally and who were capable of resolving any setting out difficulties on the site. Added to this we had the problem of working to the architect's panel layout and tie-bolt locations. Not all of the concrete for the structure was cast in place. The roof edge panel and upper south wall fascia consisted of 30 mm of sprayed concrete on insulation with mesh reinforcement. The sprayed concrete was given a smooth trowel finish to give the surface the appearance of insitu concrete. For the bathroom interior walls, panels of precast concrete 100 mm thick which had a

Central staircase.

terrazzo finish were brought to site in lengths of up to 4 m and widths of 3 m and craned into position.

The formwork used was a dense visaform shutter using a natural mineral oil release agent. The workability of the concrete mix was adjusted to suit climatic conditions. It was more workable during hot and dry weather but the cement and aggregate content remained constant. Following the casting of the sample panel we had to

Construction phase seen through the woodland entrance.

Completed outer walls.

revise the mix design quite drastically to lighten the surface colour and to reduce the blemishes and blow-holes. The blastfurnace cement content was increased and 2% of white titanium dioxide pigment was added. We used a foaming agent in the concrete to reduce the deadweight of the cantilever slab for the balcony to control end-deflections. The foamed concrete slab was

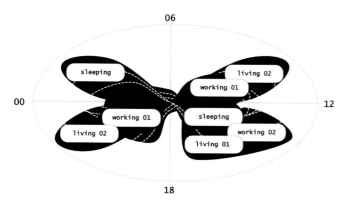

24 hour event diagram.

very porous and had to be sealed. During a heavy rain the unsealed slab soaked up a lot of moisture which took several months to dry out before the surface sealant could be applied.

The walls were poured with the use of a tremie and the concrete vibrated in even layers. The rebar was so congested in some walls that we had to use small diameter poker vibrators. On one occasion this proved impractical because the wall was on a slope, and the two 50 mm diameter poker vibrators had to be left in the wall concrete for posterity! The internal wall surfaces and internal slab soffits were water jetted and rubbed down and given a cement-wash to mask any noticeable variations in surface colour.

Ground floor living room.

Client: Anonymous
Architect: Ben van Berkel/
UN Studio
Engineer: ABT
Landscape Architect:
Adriaan Geuze
Building Contractor:
Kemmeren Bouw
Formwork:
L Keijzer
Sprayed Concrete: Vogel
Total Useable Floor Area:
550 m²; building volume
2,200 m³
Construction Phase:
17 months
Completion: 1998

Office and Home
Jo Crepain Architect, Antwerp
Jo Crepain

White-washed walls, large bay windows and soft up-lighting meets the eyes stepping in from the brick-lined familiarity of Antwerp's old town streetscape. The interior of Jo Crepain's office is chic, modern and bright, a counterpoint to the 1910 brick exterior. You forget quite quickly that the grey columns in the middle of the floor are cast iron and that this was once a coffee warehouse. The coal-black spiral staircase leading to the penthouse with its panoramic views of the River Schelde and Antwerp's gothic cathedral make you wish you could stay for the whole summer. The grey-green concrete walls are not the sleek smooth quality that was expected – photos can be deceptive – but mottled and pitted, engagingly calm and honestly reassuring: the perfect backdrop to show off Jo Crepain's collection of weird and wonderful Abstract, Kinetic and Optical Art. Furniture and art become pieces of colour floating on a canvas of grey concrete, the raking shafts of sunlight hitting the back wall add an impromptu light show for extra sensation. And one realises that concrete's intrinsic beauty can be also be drawn from its flawed and blemished imperfections.

Location
The building and loft conversion is situated on Vlaanderen Straat which is off the Schelde, in the centre of the old city of Antwerp.

Design
A disused five-storey saddleback warehouse with vaulted brick arch façade plus an adjoining nondescript two-storey building were bought for a new office and home. The five-storey building was converted into office space for 40 people on the first three floors. All the brick arches and original windows openings, even those that had been boarded up, were fully restored and double glazed. In place of the old industrial lift, a shaft of concrete rising from the basement to the roof of the fifth floor was constructed to house a central lift, staircase and service core. This structure constituted the only 'hard' volume introduced within the old building. The central core of concrete was painted entirely black except where it emerges above the fifth floor roof to house the lift motors and other service plant; it is clad in grey aluminium panels.

The living accommodation on the top two floors consists of a concrete box, with openings for windows, that is supported on the four cast iron beams within the building. The box is independent of the outer façade walls. The top of the box is a flat roof over the penthouse floor with a 4 m high ceiling. All the internal concrete surfaces were board marked using three ply-veneered douglas fir. The coarseness of the raw concrete surface interspersed with the tie-bolt holes that were arranged in an unintentional floral pattern on the walls, contrast with the silky smooth appearance of the aluminium lined widows frames, the wood flooring, the external cladding and glazing. The external face of the concrete box is clad with light grey aluminium panels. The aluminium fascia brings a fresh, bright look to an otherwise grey inner city roofscape, and works well with the tone of the restored brick façade and the dark grey render to the side and rear elevations.

The adjoining two-storey office building was demolished to make room for a much needed car park for clients, and

**Roof top apartment block
seen from the opposite bank.**

Terrace of the penthouse.

a courtyard garden. The inner garden and open car park are separated from the street by a concrete wall and a large aluminium gated entrance. A lost corner between the main building and the garden was used to build a double garage and basement for archive storage and model making. The roof of the garage was used as a terrace for the first floor dining area.

Construction

Architect's Comments: The coffee warehouse was a clean and sober building, rectangular in plan, which was ideal for both office use and residential dwelling. The internal planning was designed so that the building could be converted to flats sometime in the future if that was necessary. The office space that was introduced consists of a basement floor which contains the archives and a wine cellar, and then the ground floor which accommodates two meeting rooms, my office and studio and reception area. The first and second floors have space for up to 40 people, with a lunch room on the first floor with a terrace and the photocopy and print room on the second. The apartment begins on the third floor. It is an open space where we can hold meetings, lectures or display small art exhibitions. The guest bedrooms and our bedrooms are on this floor with a studio room for my wife. The penthouse floor is very open plan with a large lounge, kitchen and dining area and a sun terrace.

The penthouse ceiling is 4 m high. The lift room that rises above the penthouse roof initially proved a problem with the planners because it was higher than the original roof line. We were able to convince them that the set backs of the penthouse roof actually reduces the shadow line falling on the adjacent buildings, when compared to the original pitched roof that was demolished. The external face of the concrete was clad in aluminium panels in light grey – a neutral colour. The internal concrete was designed to be light grey to provide a quiet backdrop to the changing colours of furniture, fabric, clothing, art and lighting. Natural material colour – grey, white and even black – are preferred; not strong brick red colours which are too dominant. Black is not an intrusive nor offensive colour in my view and has been used here to paint the concrete staircase in the apartment and the interior walls of the lift core.

Restored brick façade.

Spiral staircase.

At the beginning of the contract a sample of concrete comprising white cement, white sand and white aggregate was made to produce a very light grey surface finish. The contractor cast a white concrete in the basement which we approved as the standard for the rest of the project. Then following further discussion, the contractor gave a number of reasons why they were nervous to use white concrete, with the wood grain finish that we had wanted on the upper floors. They said it was difficult to guarantee uniformity of colour or minimum blemishes, and on top of that the ready mixed concrete supplier was demanding a longer period of notice before delivery to site. It seems that if you want special concrete in Antwerp it is only going to be delivered at 4 pm on Friday, at the end of the working week! Moreover the contractor was told that they had to give the ready mixed company at least 48 hours notice for white concrete, and that was probably putting too much reliance on the contractor's ability to plan ahead! So we agreed that grey concrete would be acceptable.

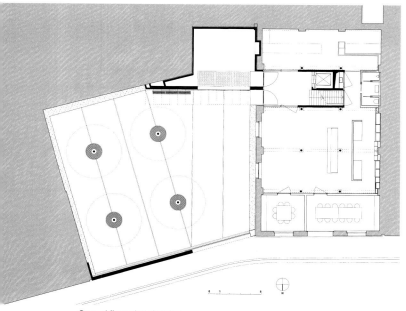

Ground floor plan showing courtyard.

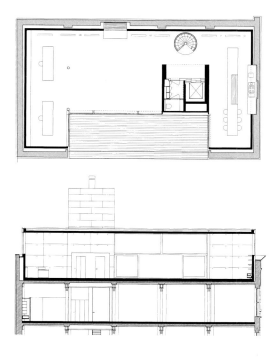

Top floor of apartment.

Section through apartment floors and roof top.

Dark grey rendered side elevation overlooking the courtyard.

After one use the ply formwork face was discarded to ensure the wood grain would imprint onto the concrete face. It was an expensive exercise. There were not many blowholes and blemishes on the feature 4 m high wall in the penthouse but as the colour did not turn out to be light grey – we rejected it. Yet the wall was not taken down, and having lived with the darker wood grained concrete now for over a year and having painted the staircase black, we have grown to like it very much.

I am reminded of a story about Alvar Aalto. An important concrete wing wall had been cast and during the pour a shutter joint had opened. When the formwork was

Original top floor construction and elevator shaft.

111

removed there was a hardened flow of concrete down the face of the wall, a big honeycombed patch and an unsightly heap of loose concrete at the base of the wall. The contractor wanted to demolish the wall. Aalto told them to leave it as it was – he felt it looked strangely beautiful and resembled a concrete lava flow. An architect should be able to accept a certain situation that is unforeseen if it adds value to the architecture.

In much the same way the honesty of the grey-green 'Crepain brut' concrete in the penthouse is preferred now to the light grey smoothness of 'Ando concrete'. It is not like any other concrete in Belgium and is unique to this building and works well with the other neutral

Original construction.

Refurbished lower apartment floor.

interior finishes. At one point we thought about grit blasting to improve the surface finish, but decided against it. Now we get phone calls from clients and other architects asking me how we achieved this particular warm grey colour to the walls! We can't tell them it was a mistake by the contractor! But this is now the quality – raw and grainy – that we wish to replicate on future projects.

A number of the tie-bolt holes were damaged or irregular in size when the formwork was removed and the entire wall in the penthouse could be seen. The contractor carried out a cosmetic repair to standardise all the tie-

Kitchen on the top floor.

bolt holes. After the holes were filled with concrete, a diamond coring machine was set up on a scaffold to core 50 mm into the concrete to make a larger hole. The hole was then filled to within 15 mm of the surface, to leave the new bolt hole feature. We paid for this extra work but we were not happy to do so.

In our experience not one contractor in Belgium is capable of producing good visual concrete that compares with the workmanship of Zumthor's architecture in Switzerland or Ando's in Japan. Most architects will specify precast concrete for these reasons, but as we do not like the faceted look of precast construction, so we will persevere with the new 'Crepain brut' warts and all.

**Lounge and high ceiling on
the top floor.**

Architect and Client:
Jo Crepain
Structural Engineer: Archidee
Contractor: Van Rijmenant nv
Gross Floor Area:
office 820 m²; apartment
340 m²
Construction Phase:
12 months
Completion: 1997

Belderbos House, Astene
Marc Belderbos

The poplars and the wild landscape shroud the deceptively long brick buildings that have been converted into a family home. Belderbos is a hands-on architect who did much of the wood work, joinery and installation of fixtures and fitting himself. Quirky art deco brick fascia hides the staggering scale of the living and working space within. The high ceiling of galvanised metal sheets, and monumental walls of warm creamy concrete, bare and blemished and feeling like old plaster, reflect the light that streams in from the window bays and window slot in the roof. It's a totally original concept, uplifting, unconventional, often untidy in detailing – there are electric wires here, there and everywhere clinging to walls or dangling overhead, the odd cobweb and do it yourself touches – but it does not matter. This place is alarmingly comfortable to be in, the views through the side windows, gable wall and even divide walls reach far out into the landscape. Belderbos has shaped and structured the land, the house, the trees, shrubs and the raised boulder roadway like a mural in the ground.

Location
The building is located in open country and can be reached by the tow path along the banks of the river Leie running through the pretty village of Astene, a suburb of Deinze. The locality is less than a half hour car journey from the city of Gent.

Design
The site was found quite by chance one day during a visit to this area to go swimming in a pond by the river Leie. Although the two single-storey industrial buildings were derelict with scrap metal and building debris strewn all about the place, the interior space was vast and had a high ceiling. We immediately thought it would be ideal for the art restoration work that my wife carries out. The open countryside, the surrounding farmland and the river location was perfect for our new home. The two industrial buildings were 60 m long and enclosed by windowless walls – the light comes from openings in the roof and windows on the gable ends. The south-facing building was 10 m wide and had a circular corrugated metal roof. It was higher than the adjoining building which was wider but had a shallow pitched roof. The steel truss rafter sections of the circular roof supports – believed to be made in the 1950s – were still in reasonable condition. With such a high roof space we naturally restored this building and turned it into an artists workshop and a home for our family. The other building has remained uninhabited and is used for storage.

The original design of the buildings was made by industrial engineers with no aesthetic, they were purpose built

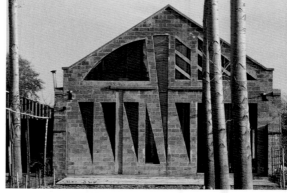

South gable.

to house workshops for fabricating and repairing dredging barges. Yet the curved roof of the south-facing building was architecturally pleasing and there was a Renaissance feel about such an enclosing structure. I had been studying architectural restoration and conservation in Italy for five years and the idea of creating an inner space of beauty enclosed by this industrial shell, evoked for me the work of the great Renaissance architects like Brunelleschi and Palladio. But instead of separating the landscape from the building we wanted to integrate the building with the landscape by cutting large window openings through the south enclosing wall.

114

The building was long and symmetrical in plan. Somehow the notion of dividing the building into regimented rectangular spaces did not appeal to us. We wanted to create some 'theatre' within the space, so we positioned the partition walls at an oblique angle to the long enclosing wall, rather than a right angle and chose an offset angle of 10 degree for setting them out. We also used this 'obliqueness' to orientate the garden walkway, paths, pond and the new tree line that has been planted in front of the house. The internal dividing walls of mass concrete reach up to the curved roof which is 7 m high at the crown. They run from the window wall and stop 1.5 m short of the inner longitudinal brick wall, to abut a new

The original site.

Illuminated south gable.

concrete corridor wall. Apart from the doorways that are built through them, each dividing wall has an internal window slot which runs from top to the bottom of the wall – the slot is wider at the top and reduces in width as it reaches the base of the wall. The slot is glass-filled and appears like a ray of light streaming in from the roof. The

115

slots become subtly wider in the walls as they near the south gable, parodying the oblique angle of the wall itself.

The building is divided by function into two halves – the living quarters and the working section. The original south-facing blockwork wall has been opened up to create a series of large window openings, framed by the original precast concrete support columns and divided by the concrete partition walls. In the workshop and studio rooms a series of concrete treads built into the dividing wall takes you up to a gallery floor with bookshelves and storage space. The wooden gallery floor is supported on steel joists that span between the dividing walls and are propped by tubular steel columns. In the living quarters, one room has a large open fire place that has been built within a concrete wall surround. A metal chimney tops the large concrete canopy slab of the fire place to direct smoke away. The second room within divide walls contains the kitchen and dining area and a gallery floor that overhangs the kitchen and encloses the bath and shower room. The slatted panel of the concrete wall that enclose the bathroom is made of alternating slender horizontal concrete beams and glass panels. A narrow wooden staircase built onto the concrete divide wall goes up to the bedroom floor and bathrooms. The bedroom floor is a mezzanine built between the divide wall and north gable. The timber floor of the mezzanine is supported on steel joists and tubular steel columns, and is braced by the gable wall and the frame of the shell building. To get light into the ground floor lounge and bedrooms above, long angular slots have been cut into the original gable wall and windows inserted. The north wall was braced by a concrete portal frame which once supported a heavy shutter door. The horizontal section of the portal had to be cut to form the long vertical slot in the wall, echoing the slotted opening in the internal walls. The windows in the gable wall are angular, emphasising the obliqueness of the internal building axis.

The curved roof itself is made up of a double skin of galvanised metal sheeting sandwiching an insulation layer and a damp proof membrane. The construction of the original building was very sound. A perimeter ground beam supported on pile foundations carries the precast concrete columns, the infill brickwork and arch roof structure. The 150 mm deep reinforced ground-supported slabs were sufficient to take the loads from the mass concrete divide walls, the corridor walls and tubular steel columns supporting the mezzanine floors.

Terracotta tiles from Italy were used for covering the ground floor in the living room. American oak was used for the wood staircase and balustrading and light grey

Mass concrete divide wall and slot.

Artist studio, gallery and galvanised metal roof.

concrete for the new walls. All these materials are primary materials which have been chosen because they do not require decoration or painting. Power points, light switches and light fitments are fixed directly to the surface of the concrete.

Construction

Architect's Comments: There were many contractors who did not understand what we were trying to do and turned us down. Fortunately we found Willie Copens who relished the challenge of building our home because he wanted to try something different. He had no previous experience of producing good visual concrete

Kitchen and dining area, steps leading to bedrooms and bathroom.

but felt confident of doing a good job. Three men built the house, and I built the wooden staircase and most of the interior fittings. For me, it was the first encounter with concrete. One major concern was the natural finish that we were trying to achieve, another was the motivation to form concrete as visually pleasing as the architecture of Tadao Ando, which has influenced me.

Then there was the consideration of cost. If we had built the dividing walls and corridor wall in brickwork, then plastered it and painted it the cost would have been higher and we would have to paint it again in the future. If we wanted the brickwork to be exposed then the workmanship would have to be far better, and the labour cost and brick quality far higher. The concrete walls are 400 mm thick; this was economic as there was no reinforcement required. The shuttering costs far more than the concrete which is only about 20% of the overall cost, so if the concrete thickness is increased one can avoid the cost of reinforcement. Moreover we did not want 'curtain' thin concrete walls designed with lots of re-inforcement – we wanted the walls to look monumental.

The contractor bought enough formwork to complete one divide wall. The formwork was taken up in two lifts to reach the top of the wall. Panel joints and tie-bolt hole positions were planned in advance. The formwork was factory cut and supplied by Comital and delivered to the site in 24 pieces. Generally it took two hours to pour each lift. Only one poker vibrator was used to compact the concrete which was pumped into the forms. We should have had at least two pokers, with one on standby in case of breakdown, to do the job effectively. The concrete mix used 250 kg of cement per cubic metre and 125 kg of hydraulic lime. The lime was added on my insistence in the belief that it would improve the surface colour and smoothness of the finish. The ready mixed company were perplexed with this instruction and asked that we should supply the lime for them to incorporate in the mix. The hydraulic lime was purchased from Lafarge in

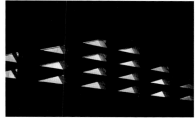

Light slots cut into new brick fascia of the adjoining building.

Brick fascia.

119

Isometric showing divide
walls and oblique grid.

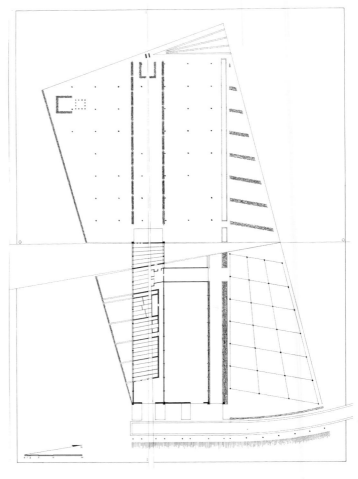

Building plan, oblique grid
and garden plan.

France in bags and sent to the local ready mixed yard. During my research work in Italy it was evident that hydraulic lime when added to cement produces a much denser and closer internal structure seen under a microscope than one with just OPC. This accounts for the durability of early Roman cements.

When the formwork was removed the finish was acceptable although there were blowholes, a few blemishes and some areas of grout loss and honeycombing. The colour was warm and there was a plaster-like feel to the surface when you worked your hand over it, but it was not the marble smooth finish that was expected. Having understood a lot more about visual concrete since the house was built, I would not attempt to specify visual concrete this way again. First of all a varnished birch-wood ply would be used for the formwork; a release agent – for instance by Pieri of France – would be specified to ensure a really good surface finish and the cement content of the mix would be 350 kg per cubic metre or more; the water cement-ratio would be limited to 0.5 and hydraulic lime would not be used. Concrete as a material is primitive and tactile like mud or wet sand that you can mould into a castle. It's a material that is honest and creates an architecture that is not mannered, that it is self-finished and without flamboyance.

Building gables seen from
the north-west.

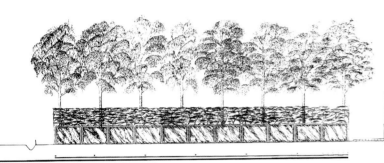

East elevation and planting
line.

Tall widows bays of the east
elevation.

Client: Belderbos Family
Architect: Marc Belderbos
Contractor: Willie Copens
Gross Floor Area: 600 m²
Project Value:
BEF 6.4 million
Construction Phase:
12 months
Completion: 1995

Sanderus Printing Factory, Oudenaarde

Christian Kieckens

Although the historic centre of Flemish Oudenaarde is pretty, the town's industrial periphery is an ugly and ill-fitting collection of shed style buildings. The architect has gone a long way to prove that good architecture, given the opportunity, can cure such shortcomings. The clean lines and open, light-filled interiors of the printing factory unify the work space and the offices but suggests that good architecture comes at a price. Yet this factory has been built for 'next to nothing' with standard precast floor planks and long span roof beams, exposed insitu concrete, timber partition walls, etched glass cladding and black finishing bricks. Kieckens' combination of brutal and blemished concrete surfaces onto which are fitted overhead lights, switches, radiators and colour coordinated pipelines and ducting, juxtaposed by vividly coloured translucent screens, doors with smooth wood finishes and painted steelwork gives this building a dynamism and informal hierarchy. Some offices are stark and bare, some are boldly coloured and richly grained, while other spaces are expansive and calming. It is minimalism with attitude. The long front elevation with its subtly varying set backs could easily be mistaken for an expensive office building. Pity the old house was not demolished to give an uninterrupted view of Kieckens' seriously playful architecture.

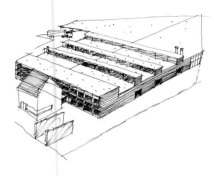

Isometric plan of building.

Location

The printing factory can be found in the industrial section of Oudenaarde 20 km from Gent along the N59, which was the old trunk road to Flanders.

Design

The printing factory is built on the site of a former building company yard. All the existing buildings were demolished except the original house which has been retained for the administrative offices. In the new scheme the ground floor of the old house has been refurbished into the reception area. It would have been better to demolish the house but the cost of the replacement was felt to be too great by the client.

The basic design had to provide the functional space required for the printing works and keep the building cost within the tight budget set by the client. However, the overall arrangements of the internal space and building form attempts to discards any preconceived notion that the building should look like a factory. The internal volume has been organised into separate zones, the first of which embodies a two-storey block fronting the length of the building which caters for current and future office space; the central single-storey wide span enclosure with its glazed canopy roof is zoned for the machinery, processing and collation hall; and the third area is a repeating two-storey block to be used for storage.

The deliberate use of standard factory made construction components and external cladding has kept the building form simple and repetitive, while the application of interior colour following close consultation with the client tries to harmonise and personalise the interior space to create a better working environment.

Construction

Architect's Comments: We wanted to design a building where the functions were not separated from the construction. The budget set for the building was extremely tight at BEF 14,750/m^2 which included all the fittings, finishes and design fees. It was natural that the choice of materials to enclose and service the building would be limited to inexpensive off the shelf building components. The idea of designing a building that had sustainability was also important. For us, this meant a capacity for expansion and adaptability to other functions if the building was to be sold.

The building layout was on a 9 m by 6 m module, with the main building 50 m by 42 m in plan, adjoining a large covered goods handling yard at the rear. Goods vehicles must use a service road adjacent to the 42 m long south elevation, to access the goods handling yard. The two-storey office block running on the eastern and western flanks of the central printing hall, are divided into 9 m by 6 m walled rooms which can be partitioned into offices with a central corridor or left open plan for storage purposes.

The central printing hall has a span of 24 m with a black brick-clad north elevation and green-blue light-filtering glass façade on the south. This Reglit glass façade allows the owner to extend the building quite easily and to reuse the modular glass panels. Profiled metal roofing over the printing hall is supported on long tapered pre-cast flanged beams, every 6 m. There is a 6 m wide, 2 m high, raised canopy roof running down the centre of the printing hall with large lightweight polycarbonate side windows to bring daylight into the factory. The end ele-

Brick-faced north elevation.

Front elevation
and existing house.

Office corridor.

Construction of divide walls and first floor slab.

vations of the printing hall have a stepped roof profile – the upper level of the step is formed by the flat roofs of the two end blocks and the top hat section of the printing hall roof, while the lower level is created by the metal roof sections resting on the tapering beams that span the printing hall. This rhythm is repeated on the façade of the western elevation but with a much smaller step between glazing boxes. This 'impression and expression' of the façade at ground floor level runs on a 12 m module. The proportions and rhythm of these features have been carefully programmed with reference to classical order. The cornice was kept proud of the window line to give a crisp edge to the roof.

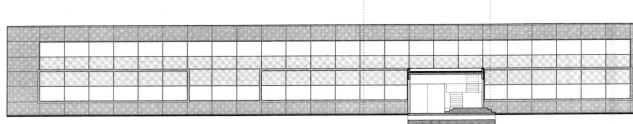

Front façade (east elevation).

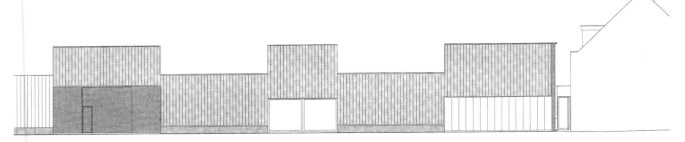

Glass panelled south elevation.

South elevation.

We designed the walls of the two offices as load-bearing block work. The suspended floors comprise 160 mm deep by 1,200 mm wide precast hollow core planks with an 80 mm concrete topping for running service pipes and ducting. The ground floor is a power floated ground supported slab with a water proof coating. The 24 m factory-made precast tapered beams are supported on separate insitu concrete columns with interconnecting beams that tie in with the load-bearing walls of the office block. Lighting cable, small bore service ducts and other conduits were detailed to be built into the hollow core masonry walls and the lights boxes, switches, radiators panel and the like to be surface-mounted.

Ground floor corridor and
service trunking.

Wide span beams and central
factory floor.

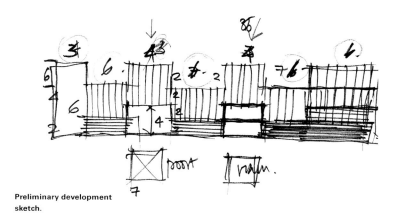

Preliminary development
sketch.

View of ceiling
with light fitting.

It came as a surprise when the contractor asked if all the
blockwork walls could be substituted for cast in place
concrete. This caused no extra cost, and even improved
construction productivity working through the winter
months. On reflection now it would have been better to
have provided more specific information in the contract
about the concrete surface finish and to have coordinated the tie-bolt hole positions and panel layout
more rigorously.

Coloured panels in doorway.

Protruding window line of ground floor office block.

Contractor's Comments: The formwork panels were prefabricated and supplied by Comital. They had a plywood face backed with aluminium stiffeners. The panels were assembled in 3.8 m high by 9 m long sections for the dividing walls in the two-storey office and storage blocks. Box outs for the access corridor, doorway or other openings were made within the wall formwork. The release agent used was a product called 'Rewah' which we use regularly. The release agent was applied to the form face by spray gun before the rebar was positioned. It has good adhesion and is active for 48 hours and does not wash off when it rains. Sufficient formwork was ordered to make two sets of 9 m long wall shutters. The tie-bolts holes and panel layout positions were agreed with the architect in advance.

The concrete was supplied by Société OBC, a subsidiary of Interbeton, from a ready mixed plant nearby. The architect asked for an F3 finish which requires

Bare finishes to interiors.
Precast concrete panels on external face.

'a smooth finish, uniform in texture and appearance with formwork that does not lead to blemishes.' Though the finish that resulted with the formwork system and concrete mix was not F3, it was accepted by the architect who took a pragmatic and realistic overview of what could be achieved within the budget price of the contract. The 200 mm thick walls were cast without kickers and the concrete was placed by skip and discharged through a short tremie pipe into the formwork. The skip was moved along the length of the wall by mobile crane to ensure an even spread of concrete. Each divide wall required 7 m^3 of concrete and was poured in three lifts and internally vibrated. Two divide walls were cast every second day and in all about 400 m^3 of concrete was used to complete them.

The precast planks for the suspended floors followed two weeks after the walls were cast on the ground floors. Then the 80 mm screed layer was pumped and levelled over the precast units once the service pipework had been laid. On the roof the screed was laid to falls onto which insulation panels were placed and covered by three layers of roofing felt. Work progressed steadily and our only problems related to the co-ordination of the electrical and mechanical service ducts which had to be fixed within the walls and proved very labour-intensive. The box out for light switches and other small openings on the form face had to be carefully positioned to level and line. We wanted to avoid having to diamond core the wall because a vital service duct had been forgotten. The ground supported slab was cast and power floated when the central roof span over the printing hall was in place so that the flooring team were under cover and concrete was protected from any sudden drop in temperature or burst of rainfall which would ruin the finish.

Client: Drukkerij Sanderus nv
Architect: Christian Kieckens with Kristoffel Boghaert, Koen Drossaert and Piet Crevits
Engineer: Studiobureau Koen de Klerk Engineering
Contractor: Alheembouw nv
Interiors: Houtconstructio Wyckaert
Surface Area: 4,300 m^2
Project Value: BEF 73 million
Construction Phase: 12 months
Completion: 1996

**Morella School, Morella,
Castellón de la Plana**
Carme Pinós & Enric Miralles

Cut into the hillside, terraced like rice fields, the school sits sheltering beneath the gaze of the old moorish castle and walled town of Morella. The angled geometry of the walls and complexity of the internal levels of this three-dimensional jigsaw maximise the orientation of each façade towards the light. The vertical blades of precast concrete acting as diffusers of direct sunlight, add drama and composition to an otherwise plain façade. The cluster of buildings and their function can be identified more easily from their roof top plan or choice of roofing material – corten steel over the assembly hall roof, a zig-zag layout for the flat roofs of the dormitory block and so on. Concrete has been used for the structure and archi-tecture, insitu concrete for the frame, and precast con-crete for the cladding. The colourful wooden window and doorway frames, the bright metal doors and railing set within their concrete surround, bring a vibrancy to the building architecture.

Location

The ancient walled town of Morella is dominated by the ruins of a Moorish castle built around a large rock out-crop that is one of the high points of the valley. Morella's colourful history and dramatic hilltop location make it a popular tourist attraction. It is 60 km from Vinaroz travelling towards the del Maestrazgo mountains, on the N232. The school is situated on the southern slopes outside the town walls and directly below the old castle.

Design

It is impossible not to remember mythical geological configurations like the image of a giant or a beast petrified in the rock face when working in Morella. The old Moorish city itself works for me as a sundial, with streets that look like cuts made in the mountain side and orientated to give the best possible light. The model of the school that we made for the construction tries to capture the best orientation for the light in much the same way.

Working with all our senses, not just vision, we wanted to discover Morella – the rhythm of the landscape, the orientation of the light, and the shadows of the mountain. The building we designed is a boarding school for children in the region. The programme comprises teaching rooms, laboratories, a library, hall, communal dining room, leisure room with TV and games, gymna-sium, and small theatre. It also contains a kindergarten and conference hall for community use. There is a munici-pal swimming pool close to the school which can be used by the pupils and teaching staff.

This is a design that responds to the colours, vibrations and moods of the surrounding countryside. We spent many hours looking over the area where the school was to be located, studying the citadel and familiarising ourselves with the tracks that mark out the territory.

It was upon first impulse that we decided to make the building outline a series of terraces that follow the rising contours – weaving in and out of the mountainside. It is important that the architecture of Morella School must not dominate the landscape nor compete with the famous citadel which overlooks it nor scar the unspoilt countryside. Many details contribute to this: the window shutters, the vertical screens and the changing angle of the façade, from elevation to elevation.

Construction

Architect's Comments (Carme Pinós): Photographs were taken of the area from every possible perspective. For example to the south looking up we see the citadel, to the east the skyline is dominated by rows of houses with red tiled roofs and so on. The orientation of the building spaces are angled and turned in a deliberate way to respond to these changing scenes. Seen from the citadel the structure is retracted into the mountainside. Seen from within the building, the internal space reaches out into the landscape. The separation walls between rooms and buildings are angled to catch the morning light but screened from the fierce mid-day sun by vertical precast

Teaching block façade with blades of precast blinds.

blades acting as blinds. The collection of buildings are on split levels. The levels cascade down the sloping site as terraces.

The fragmented building plan with its changing angles and levels, was going to make construction difficult. A model of the building was made which could be broken down into elemental sections to show how every wall, floor and roof linked together. Detailed drawings of each wall section was prepared and referenced on the model, to give the contractor as much help as needed to build what the architect had designed.

The dormitory block was arranged like a cluster of houses, in zigzag fashion, separated from the teaching block and conference building. The boarders should not have to feel they are forever in the same 'classroom' environment. Each building within the school was different in orientation and architectural treatment. The prominent roof of the conference hall between the class rooms, laboratories and library is covered in corten steel panels

Constructing the walls of the dormitory block.

The student 'dormitory' building and upper terrace.

130

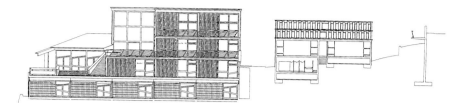

Garden elevation of teaching
block, with dormitory on
right-hand side.

Model for construction.

meant to give an earth colour as the steel tarnishes. The façade of the classroom block is a series of alternating storey-high glazing panels – the larger windows are surrounded in painted wooden frames, while the smaller ones are framed by closely spaced 'blades' of precast concrete. The dormitory block features a long, repeating row of storey-high window openings, each one framed in painted wood and separated by slender blades of precast concrete.

We chose concrete for its organic and plastic properties and because it was the economic choice in this remote area. The concrete was tinted with yellow pigment to create a natural stone colour similar to the rock in the region. A number of sample panels were cast with different pigment concentrations and pigment combinations and were stood in the sun to decide the most appropriate finished colour. The building structure, the flat roof, main dividing walls and perimeter walls are insitu concrete. The perimeter walls are covered by precast panels and insulation. We had to do this to avoid cold bridging through the insitu wall. Thin precast panels, 450 mm by 650 mm in plan size, are arranged like paving flags in angled rows running across the face of the external wall and colour matched to the insitu concrete.

We used birchwood doors and panels to the stud frame partitions. Internal blockwork walls are rendered and white washed. We designed the interiors, detailing all the fixtures, furniture and all the fittings.

During construction of the retaining wall on the upper slopes, there was a landslip, and this undermined the foundations. A deeper excavation was made to anchor the wall into more stable ground. The condition was

caused by a slip during a prolonged period of wet weather. Loose rubble fill had been dumped here over many years from the town excavations. It was apparently not picked up during the soil investigation.

Contractor's Comment: This project was very demanding and complex. It did not make our job any easier when we were advised by the architect that the design was not finalised when we were about to start on site. At the time of tender the architect only provided a general idea of the construction, without specific working details. We were told that the tender information only gave the intentions of the architecture, which was sufficient for pricing purposes but not for construction! Detailed drawings are issued once on site. This means that the architect can alter and adapt the work during construction without penalty. It is not good practice but is typical of contractual conditions in Spain.

Formwork layout and details were drawn up by us on site and then sent to the architect for comment, revision and approval. Wall forms were supplied by Peri in 625 mm by 1,250 mm, 625 mm by 2,500 mm and 1,250 mm by 2,500 mm sizes. The formwork panels were covered with a bonded phenolic sheet to improve surface finish. There was no guidance on the concrete colour or the mix. Numerous concrete samples were made before the

Internal corridor and staircase.

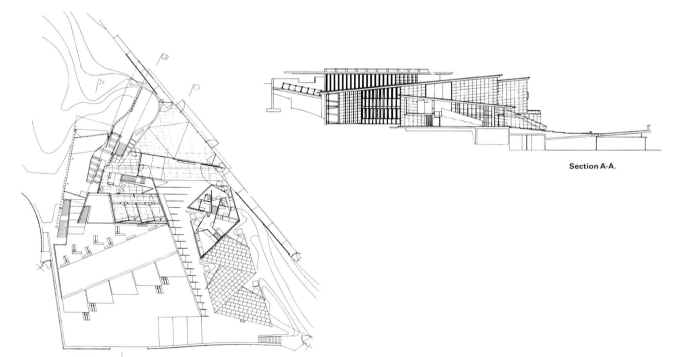
Section A-A.

Building plan.

Lower terrace with citadel in background.

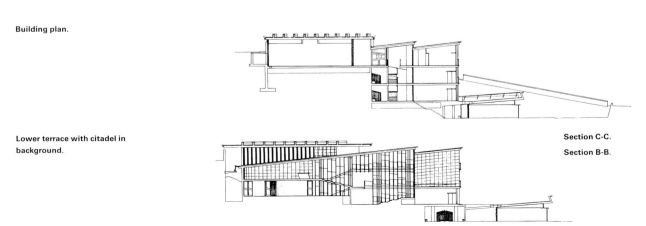
Section C-C.

Section B-B.

133

Dining room.

Doorway.

External staircase, dormitory
block.

colour was agreed and concrete could be supplied. This was time consuming and expensive.

The insitu concrete was batched and mixed on site because Morella was in such a remote location. The precast panels, the vertical blade units, paving slabs and external concrete seats were produced in a factory in Vinaroz. The plant on site had a batch capacity of one cubic metre. Two 50 tonnes cement silos were installed to ensure there were no problems with deliveries during the winter months when road conditions become treacherous. Coarse aggregates were heated and the formwork and exposed concrete surface covered with thick canvas for curing. Concreting was stopped if the air temperature was likely to drop below 5 degree C. The insitu concrete mix comprised 320 kg/m^3 of grey OPC, with 890 kgs of 20–6 mm aggregates and 930 kgs of sand. The water-cement ratio was kept at 0.50 to give the concrete reasonable workability, while maintaining durability. Yellow pigment was dosed at 1.15 % of cement content. Precast

Client: Patrimonio /
Generalitat Valenciara
Architect: Carme Pinós &
Enric Miralles
Structural Engineer: Obiols
Services Engineer: Jordi
Altes
Contractor: Dragados
Building Area: 2,100 m^2
Project Value: Pts. 600 million
Construction Phase:
24 months
Completion: 1994

units were made with white cement with yellow pigment added at 1.15% of cement content. They were cast in metal forms and strengthened with fabric reinforcement.

Before concreting the formwork panels were cleaned and oiled. Joints were sealed with silicon. The slab formwork was covered with 10 mm thick melamine board which was replaced after each pour. Compaction of the concrete was carefully controlled to avoid poker burns to the melamine board. Surface blemishes and imperfections were repaired with a pigmented cement-resin mortar.

The first insitu wall that was cast was partially demolished on the architects' instructions because of some honeycombing and surface imperfections. We did not want to break the wall out as it was buried below ground level and could have been repaired.

Night view.

Fuencarral Library, Madrid

Andrés Perea Ortega

The jewel-box light shaft columns slicing futuristically through the floors of the library, surrounded by shiny wall to wall coverings, might be mistaken for a swanky concert hall, a Gucci fashion house or even the bridge of the Enterprise in Star Trek, but never a library. The sloping upper floors could be a touch irritating if you dropped your marbles or some loose change to watch them roll and roll and roll. Overall the light-filled spaciousness of the library is as inspired as the glass-walled exit corridors slotted into the corners of the building. Although there would appear to be a decided lack of concrete on display inside the building, there is a glut of it wrapping the outside of it – rough, brutal and raw. It takes a little getting used to. The coloured windows and light slots cut into the concrete façade, and provide relief to an otherwise bland wall. The expansive glass elevation of the main entrance brings huge gulps of light into the building.

Location

The District of Fuencarral in Madrid lies to the north of the city, about 20 minutes by car. The library can be found on San Jenjo Street.

Design

The marked incline of the ground, the vacant trapezoidal plot and lack of buildings in the immediate neighbourhood, suggested the possibilities of an unusual architecture. The new library building has been conceived as an inward looking container, with the internal spaces turned towards the central core of the built volume. The process of introversion, of focusing on the central atrium and courtyard, is heightened by the ceilings of the upper floors slanting inwards towards the central courtyard. This inward slope attains its greatest magnitude on the roof which is shaped like an inverted pyramid.

The result of this process is the conception of a building as a vast trapezoidal prism enclosed by concrete walls,

South façade.

137

Emergency exit and
staircase corridor.

whose only direct relationship with the outside is limited to the glass-fronted west elevation and glass-walled central atrium. Natural light is also brought in from the east and south elevations into the heart of the working space, by glass-panelled lattice frame structures.

The main entrance on the west elevation is at the lowest level of the plot. The main staircase leads up to the entrance from a wide street level piazza and arrives in the large inner vestibule after passing through the double glass curtain walls of the west elevation. On the first floor, which corresponds with the entrance level, the principal façade gives way to the general lobby of the library. It has been planned with a cylindrical staircase

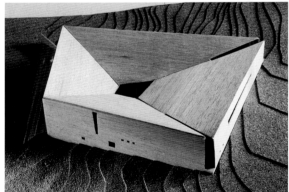

Inverted pyramid roof.

Model of structure with
principle opening slots.

that clearly delineates the access to the upper floors from the main entrance. Both the first and upper floor rooms are arranged around the central atrium that can be accessed from the walkway surrounding it.

The inner space of the building adopts a radial organisation. This radial arrangement, with the rooms and spaces separated only by glazed screens, gives visual continuity to all the floors. On the entrance floors are the newspaper library, the children's reading rooms, a lecture theatre and spaces for audio-visual presentation and group activities. The rooms that demand privacy such as the administrative offices and toilets are tucked away to the sides of the main lobby to avoid breaking the

West elevation and main entrance.

visual continuity of the inner space. The second floor is dedicated to the reading and study rooms. The reading desks are situated on wooden platforms equipped with locating sockets to overcome the slight slope of the floor.

Construction

Architect's Comments: The big difference in levels between the upper street on the eastern boundary and lower street on the western side and the more gentle slope across the north-south axis gave us the opportunity to make this a feature of the building. The trapezoidal plan evolved by following the line of the site boundary. We could have made this building a regular cubic struc-

Aerial view of site.

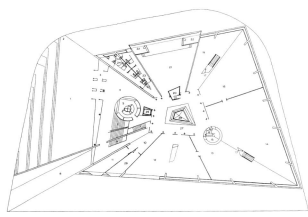

First floor plan.

ture with level floors and a flat roof but it would not have had the same interest. The split wall on the south-east corner of the building for example forms a staircase corridor leading to the upper street level. It adds interest as well as brings light into the upper floor.

We chose concrete because we wanted the building structure to be monolithic from foundation to the roof. As there was a large excavation to be dug and retaining walls to be built to hold back the ground along the high points of the site, concrete was the natural choice. To change to another structural material above ground would be dishonest and rather false in our view. The retaining wall below ground continues above ground to

Construction of south elevation.

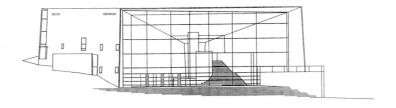

West elevation.
South elevation.

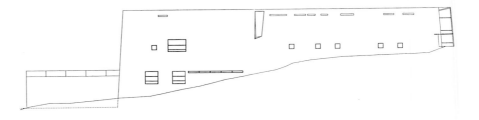

become solid façade walls of the library superstructure. The surface finish to the exposed concrete to the external walls was not what we had originally wanted. Various discussions took place between the contractor and ourselves about the finishes and in the end we opted to leave the walls as they were with a rough cast, brutal finish. It expresses the panel joints, bolt holes, grout runs and blemishes to show that the walls were made by workmen on this site. We did not want any render or cosmetic paint to mask the intrinsic quality of such an organic construction. The synthetic, manufactured look of precast concrete has no character.

Sample panels were made with concrete batched from a small portable mixer on site. The samples were unreal because we believed that such a smooth blemish free finish could not be achieved with the formwork panels and ready mixed concrete that the contractor had priced for. The way concrete specifications are interpreted in this region of Spain, means it only binds the contractor to satisfy the structural performance standards for the concrete. Any guidance notes that we put into the specification on the production of visual concrete can be ignored because it is not legally enforceable. Of course we wanted a smooth, blemish free surface finish to the concrete. Publicly funded projects like Fuencarral are procured by competitive tender and awarded to the lowest bidder. As architects we provide concept drawings, a specification and bill of quantities for the contractor to price. What invariably happens is that the contractor only prices for those items that are contractually binding to keep costs down. We did get the contractor to paint the inside walls of the building to even out surface discoloration and to hide large blemishes. The contractor also wanted to coat the exterior concrete face to hide the imperfections, but we refused.

Entrance hall.

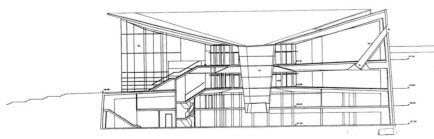

Section: east - west.

Section: north - south.

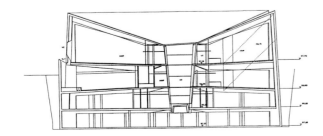

141

Trapezoidal light box
bringing daylight from
window slot in east elevation
wall.

Basement construction and
internal columns.

Concrete pyramid roof during
construction.

A few sections of retaining wall had to be broken out and
rebuilt because the concrete either failed to meet the
strength required or the cover to the reinforcement was
inadequate for durability. It was never rejected for
aesthetic reasons.

The shiny floor, wall and ceiling panels are actually MDF
boards which have been lacquered and made fireproof.
The smooth, factory made wood finish of the MDF
sheeting and floor tiles contrast with the rough cast
finish of the exterior concrete. The material was difficult
to source in Spain but we found a manufacturer in
Portugal. If the surface of the floor tiles gets tarnished
over a period of time they are cheap and easy to replace.
We accounted for this in assessing the long term maintenance costs of the building.

Contractor's Comments: We did not receive any guidance notes with the tender document on the finishes to the concrete. That came later once we were on site and were asked to make samples. In the contract there was only the structural concrete performance notes to base our price on. In allowing the architect to decide and approve the finish and colour of the sample panel, the concrete mix and formwork cost can escalate. So it's possible that with every cubic metre we are placing we could be losing money. The architect on this occasion was very understanding of the situation and accepted the structural concrete finish that we had priced for.

Central courtyard.

Sloping ceiling, lacquered mdf floor and radial plan.

The structural concrete that was purchased for the contract was clearly not adequate for producing visual concrete. As the acceptability of concrete is strength based, the ready mixed supplier will use a water reducing admixture to minimise the cement content of the mix and a retarder to delay the set of the concrete when it is batched in hot summer periods. If we are asked to produce visual concrete in the future, we will need a precise specification with the tender documents giving clear guidance on what the architect wants to achieve. On this project we would have priced for a much richer cement mix and substituted birchwood ply for the formwork for achieving a good surface finish, instead of the phenolic board that we used.

Client: Consejeria de Cultura, Comunidad de Madrid.
Architect: Andrés Perea Ortega
Technical Architect: Fernando Ruiz Hervas
Structural Engineer: Indagsa
Services Engineer: Juan Izquierdo Engineers
General Contractor: Pefersan, SA
Total Floor Area: 4,572 m^2
Project value: Pts. 520 million
Construction Phase: 36 months
Completion: 1998

Design images of courtyard access.

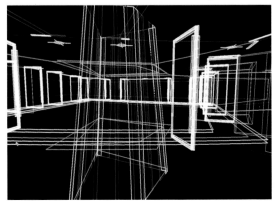

Tulach a'tSolais,
Oulart Hill,
County Wexford
Ronnie Tallon
and Michael Warren

The memorial is on the brow of a gently rising hill that is hidden from view. There are not many signs encouraging tourists to find it either. Many of the local residents would prefer this unspoilt part of County Wexford to remain unchanged, with the memorial left untouched and not overrun with tourists. Persistence will be rewarded. The walk from the makeshift car park to the memorial takes you along a path bordering the field where the Irish ambushed the English on May 27 in 1798. The Mound of Oulart beckons in the distance, the clean white walls of the inner structure glow bright in any light. The split of the walls framing the memorial chamber, opens up a view of Vinegar Hill 10 km away to make a dramatic and poignant statement. The first Irish Republic lasted for just three weeks – the time it took them to win the first battle here on Oulart Hill and to lose the last on Vinegar Hill on June 21 in 1798. The walls of the chamber are marble white insitu concrete, precisely formed and very fair-faced. The grass covered mound that the walls retain is a vivid green carpet, restful and calming in the surrounding meadow grass and cluster of newly planted trees. The cast in place concrete is workmanship of the highest order. The two plinths of sculptured 200-year-old oak resting symbolically on the chamber floor, the work of a consummate artist.

Location
The Oulart memorial can be found by taking the N11 south of Dublin. A signpost along the N11 about 100 km from Dublin and 30 km from Wexford will take you along a narrow road leading past Oulart village and onto to the memorial car park. A short walk along a ridge towards Oulart Hill brings you to Tulach a'tSolais – the Mound of Light.

Design
Tulach a'tSolais – the Mound of Light – was designed to commemorate the United Irish Rising in a considered and inclusive context. The memorial places the uprising of 1798 in its true international perspective and what historians commonly call the Atlantic Revolution of France and America. The project enshrines the events of 1798 within the Enlightenment period, with a particular focus on the first attempt to establish a popular democracy in Ireland.

The memorial comprises a large landscaped mound, separated by two retaining walls along a central east-west axis. The split in the walls symbolises the gap between the feudal era and the new democratic age of Enlightenment. The walls define the passageway that passes through the recessed chamber within the mound. By careful calculation the alignment of the walls allows the inner chamber to receive the maximum illumination on June 21, which is the Summer Solstice and the date of the battle of Vinegar Hill. Looking up from within the open passageway, the viewer will see a long strip of sky framed by the retaining walls. Collite Eireann who own the woodlands around Oulart agreed to cut a swathe 11 m wide by 170 m long through the mature trees along the slopes of the east-west axis, to give a clear view to Vinegar Hill.

The inner chamber is paved with bush hammered granite flags and has white concrete enclosing walls. Within the chamber there are two pieces of 200-year-old Irish oak designed by sculptor Michael Warren. The solid chunks of

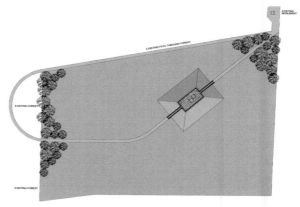

Plan of scheme.

timber curve gently upwards as though in response to the light, in deference to their intrinsic weight and rigidity. Their placement within the chamber has been determined by golden section. Overall every aspect of the monument's design has been directed towards enhancing contemplative reflection.

Construction

Architect's Comments: We had been searching for sites outside County Wexford after having found out that the land on Oulart Hill was in private ownership. But quite unknown to us a local history group in Wexford had been promised the site by the landowner and were now

Memorial chamber walls frame the view to Vinegar Hill.

looking for someone to design them a wonderful memorial. The sum of £150,000 was raised by private donation to match the funds offered by the Irish Millennium Commission to allow construction of the memorial to go ahead.

The notion of a large mound developed after we had explored and rejected the idea of building a circular shape or an underground structure. A tulach ties in well with place and history, with ancient burial mounds and Neolithic stone circles. The alignment of the two hills on the east-west axis naturally led to the idea of splitting the mound structure. The choice of white concrete gave us a clean light colour symbolising the pallor of death and the

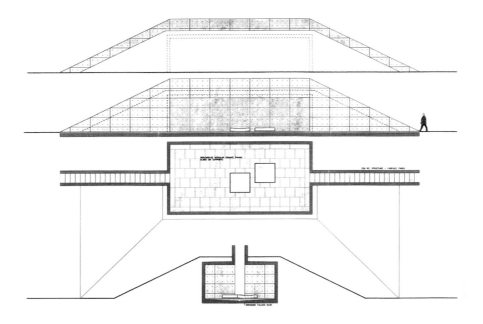

Elevation, longitudinal section, plan and cross section.

light of resurrection; of past events linked with the future. We were also determined not to clad the structure in some 'precious' local stone. We wanted a basic monolithic material of strength and nobility, with which to create a modern Stonehenge.

We decided it was better not to go to open tender but seek out the best contractor for the job and negotiate a price with them. Tender documents were prepared and a budget agreed with the cost consultant before we approached Pierse Construction. As far as we were concerned they were the best contractors in Ireland for this work with direct experience of fair-face concrete and bespoke construction.

Contractor's Comments: Initially we looked at ways of precasting the structure to achieve the surface finish quality that was wanted, but because of the remoteness of the site and poor access this proved to be impractical. The visual concrete specification prepared by the engineers Ove Arup was helpful in giving us guidance on suitable mix proportions for producing white concrete, on the use of a chemical release agent and on re-vibrating the top layer of concrete. The architect understood that money had to be spent on buying in good quality formwork and in the batching a uniformly white, ready mixed concrete. The cost of white concrete was £200/m^3

which was high because we had to cover the supplier's loss in earnings for dedicating the plant to white concrete production for the day. At peak demand times between 10 and 20 m³ of concrete was wanted in a day. It was important to dedicate the plant to white concrete production to ensure good colour consistency between batches. Storage bins, hoppers, conveyor belts, and feed pipes had to be washed and cleaned of all traces of grey concrete or non-specified aggregates. Truck mixer drums had to be thoroughly cleaned and washed out, separate storage bins had to be filled with 20 mm and 10 mm graded coarse aggregate and white sand before white concrete production could be started.

Casting the white concrete retaining walls.

For compacting the concrete, a high frequency electrically powered poker vibrator made in Germany was used, supplied by Wacker. This gives a better radius effect and more consistent compaction over the immersed length of the poker; than a conventional, mechanically driven poker vibrator. Visaform ply-faced panels were

Memorial interior.

used for the fair-face finish to the retaining walls. The architect had specified that the facing panels were to be cut to form 900 mm high by 1,800 mm long sections and each panel drilled with eight tie-bolt holes in two rows of four. The panels joint lines had to form continuous bands along and around the chamber walls. The panels were factory cut and drilled to their precise geometry in a workshop in Dublin and then shipped to the site. The shuttering system was designed and supplied by Peri (UK). When the equipment arrived in Oulart a representative from Peri spent time with the carpenters explaining how the components fitted together. Once the Peri system was in place, the Visaform panels were positioned and each one was joint sealed and secretly nailed to guard against any grout loss. All nail holes were filled and sanded before the release agent was applied. The selected release agent had to be compatible with the anti-graffiti coating that was to be applied when the concrete had hardened. Construction joints were kept within the return corner of the wall to avoid forming them on an open length of wall. The largest single pour was for the 2.7 m high by 250 mm thick walls running the length of the chamber. It needed 12 m³ of concrete to fill and took one and a half hours to pour using a mobile crane and 1 m³ skip.

Formwork in position for casting the second dividing wall.

There were very few blemishes or blowholes to the concrete surface; the only real problem occurred when large blowholes appeared on the top of the sloping section of wall built for the trial panel. After consultation with the Irish Concrete Society, a geotextile filter membrane, manufactured by Dupont Nemours and called a 'zemdrain', was installed and this proved very

The design team: Michael Warren (left), Ronnie Tallon (centre), Brian Foley (right).

View of the memorial mound from the north.

successful. There were no further blowholes but the surface was left with a cloth-like finish.

The floor of the chamber and passageway was covered with 900 mm square, 50 mm thick flags of bush hammed granite, supported on a reinforced concrete subfloor that was laid to falls. The base of the mound was made with compacted hardcore which was then covered with a geotextile membrane before backfill from the retaining wall excavation was laid and a grass layer placed over the top. A 1200 gauge bituthene layer with 12 mm thick cork protection was laid against the wall to eliminate seepage into the chamber. At the base of both retaining walls a land drain discharges any build up of rainwater run-off, away from the structure.

We used our most experienced team of men to build this project. The pride and care they took in their work is very evident in the fine surface finish of the concrete. The steel fixers plumbed every vertical bar with a spirit level to get things to fit precisely into position. Quality checks at each stage of the forming cycle ensured that shutters were clean and accurately aligned, rebar properly fixed and that any minor defect or damage to a Visaform panel meant removal and replacement with new material. It was not the cost but the quality of the finished concrete that dictated our approach on this project.

Entering the memorial chamber.

Client: Oulart Hill Co-Operative Society
Architect: Ronnie Tallon, Scott Tallon Walker and sculptor Michael Warren
Project Management: Office of Public Works, Dublin
Structural Engineer: Ove Arup Ireland
Cost Consultant: Kerrigan Sheanon Newman
Contractor: Pierse Construction.
Project Value: IEP 376,000
Construction Phase: 6 months
Completion: 1998

Vivid and calming, a symbol of remembrance and renewal.

The Ark, Temple Bar, Dublin

Shane O'Toole
and Michael Kelly
Group 91 Architects

Temple Bar is the centre of night life in Dublin, with more pubs, bars, bistro and restaurants per street than anywhere in Ireland. The Ark is situated in the heart of this lively area, its rear façade fronting onto a pedestrianised square that is the venue for regular outdoor performances and a weekend food market. The Ark as a building is a great piece of architecture with light-filled spaces, gallery walkways, open staircases, basement rooms for theatre equipment, a roof terrace, and the intimacy of a 150 seat theatre within it. The theatre metamorphoses into an open air stage when the folding metal doors on the rear elevation open on to Meeting House Square. There is contrast with old and new building façades, old brick and new concrete, steel and wood fabrication, movement and colour to sustain the delight of discovery and surprise as you wonder through it. The Ark as a children's theatre and cultural centre has achieved everything that it was designed to do.

Location

Temple Bar is the tourist centre of Dublin, an area just outside the original city walls and extending along the south bank of the Liffey. The Ark, about 200 m from the river, occupies one side of a new square bounded by the National Photographic Archive, the Gallery of Photography, the Irish Film Center and Eden Restaurant.

Design

The Ark is Europe's first purpose built cultural center for children. Since its completion it has become a case study for various European delegations wishing to develop similar facilities in their own cities.

The Ark occupies the site of a former 1725 Presbyterian Meeting House, which had been used for much of this century as a printing works and warehouse. The original interior fittings, floor beams and roof covering were removed decades ago and the building shell had stood in dereliction ever since. Apart from the plan outline of the Meeting House, the only part of the original structure that has been retained in the new building is the six-bay brick façade to Eustace Street. The design plan of the Ark, with its long entrance hall, galleried meeting rooms and staircases at both ends, was based on the original plan of the Meeting House which was discovered from an old 1843 OS Map.

A concrete façade addresses the 18 m long brick wall of the old building from which a new structural rhythm is derived. The structure of the new building is an insitu concrete frame into which is inserted the oak drum of the theatre itself. The volume of the original attic space in the roof has been reinterpreted as a north-light studio workshop with long-span concrete beams supporting upstand concrete walls concealed behind the front parapet, roof cladding and brick clad elevation.

Conservation work included stripping away the 19th century exterior render to expose the decayed old brickwork of the Eustace Street façade, then wigging and tuck pointing and rebuilding the parapet wall. More than 22 layers of paint were removed from the original Portland stone window surrounds. Retention of the original façade which had bowed, required extensive temporary works before it could be supported by the new internal concrete box structure. Existing calp limestone footings and foundations were carefully cut back and underpinned. Much of this work was carried out

Curving glass wall and seating in the attic conservatory.

Meeting House Square and redevelopment.

Folding curtain door that opens onto Meeting House Square.

Building the new concrete frame.

below the existing water table. The site abuts a long-lost watercourse which was discovered during archaeological explorations.

The Ark's new façade onto Meeting House Square is also faced in brick and stone, but its non-structural intent is revealed by being suspended, so it hovers just above pavement level of the Square. The metal folding 'stage curtain' that opens up for outdoor performances and dominates the rear elevation, was modeled on the famous warehouse doors at Coesfeld-Lette. The formal variation to adapt the folding screen for the Ark was generously suggested by Santiago Calatrava. The folding

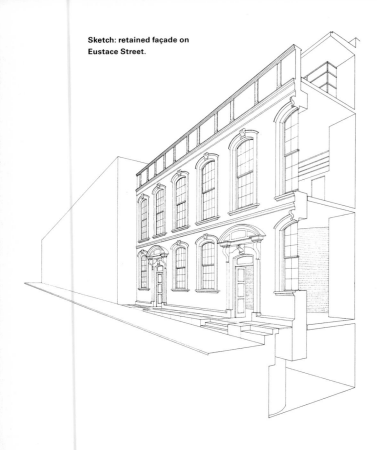

Sketch: retained façade on
Eustace Street.

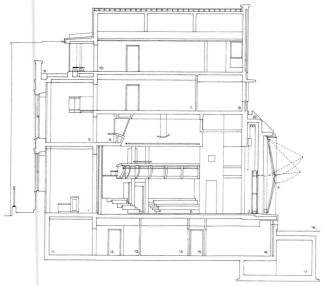

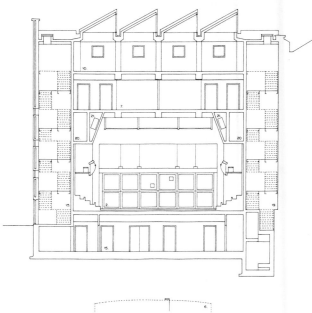

Cross section.

Longitudinal section.

Ground floor plan.

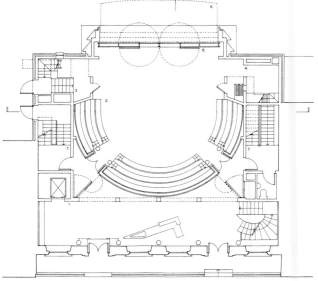

Entrance foyer.

The theatre.

doors are housed within an attached copper bellows. Stale air from the theatre is drawn out through the 'bellows' plenum, and from the gallery it is exhausted above the office window canopies.

Internally the dominant materials and finishes are 250-year-old brickwork, insitu concrete with several types of cast finish, oak, limestone, terracotta and both galvanised and oiled steel. The choice of natural, durable materials was governed by the desire to imbue the Ark with civic qualities. By restricting the use of applied colour – a red, varnished, perforated plywood lining – to the interior of the 150 seat theatre, its effect is heightened, evoking associations with an older tradition of popular auditoria.

Construction

Architect's Comments: We always felt that the building should be formed with concrete – as a material it has permanency and nobility and 'leaves a good ruin' as they say. We were aware that probably no contractor in the UK or Ireland had ever achieved the quality of insitu concrete the quality of Ando or Kahn buildings. There were a few examples of fine concrete buildings in Dublin – for example the work of architects John M Johansen and ABK in the 1960s, A & D Wejchert and Arthur Gibney a decade later, and Allies and Morrison's British Embassy

Formwork for circular staircase.

Basement corridor leading to changing rooms and plant room.

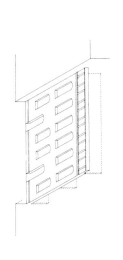

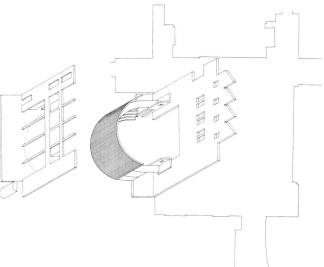

Arrangement of retained façade, internal frame and back elevation.

Building that was under construction. Having seen the British Embassy Building we made a note of the sub-contractor and agreed that the finishes would be acceptable for the Ark.

To get some measure of control of the cost – remember we had to build the theatre for just £2.4 million – we identified those areas of the concrete structure that would be finely exposed and those that were of secondary importance and put this information on a drawing. The finely exposed concrete faces were the internal 'façade' wall fronting the theatre as you enter the building – as it rose through the full height of the building – the lift shaft and open stairwell at opposite each ends of the ground floor, the double-storey high columns securing the old brick façade on Eustace Street and the open plan attic space. The building grid was based on the bay width of the old façade and consisted of six 3 m bays. The useable space within the building was four bays wide, with stair and lift access, toilets, plant and corridors occupying the end bays. The triple-height auditorium is on the ground floor and above that there are two floors, one with space for exhibitions and the other an art room studio workshop in the attic with 11.5 m long concrete beams to create a column free space. A north light to the roof brings daylight into the studio. The concrete finish on the ground floor structure which wanted to be as beautiful as possible, did not achieve the standard established by reference to a sample panel and was not as good as the finish that was achieved later in the attic. Whilst the overall visual effect is acceptable, given the contrast with the brickwork, timber and other chosen materials, it has been a big disappointment not to have achieved the desired fine finish to the concrete in the entrance lobby area

The concrete specification on surface finishes was taken from BS8110. A sample panel was cast by the contractor which set the standard of concrete finish for the job. The difficulty arose after the forms were struck on the lift shaft wall, staircase and columns on the ground floor. We rejected the concrete because it did not match the sample panel – there were noticeable dark and light patches and areas full of blowholes. The columns were cast in three lifts and there were three shades of grey, banding the columns. We even suggested that the column should be cast in one lift to avoid this happening but our advice was ignored. The contractor refused to take the concrete down and insisted that a repair could be carried out as stated in the specification. As architects we felt that a repair would look even worse and we were against this proposal. There was an impasse.

The upshot of it was that the contractor did not take down the rejected concrete and effected a cosmetic repair to the lift shaft wall. We took the view that we wanted a healthy, working relationship with the contractor if we wanted the project to finish on time and within budget. The contract was running behind schedule because of ground water problems in the basement and we did not want to fuel a further delay. In hindsight the concrete specification should have been written not allowing any making good. By accepting the substandard concrete in the ground floor, we insisted that the finish to the attic studio had to be first class. The contractor pulled out all the stops for the finishes to the difficult studio roof. We were not disappointed with the results – the finish is as good as any we have seen, anywhere.

Contractor's Comments: The contract drawings and specification were well described. We made changes to the architect's formwork panel layouts and to the box outs to be cast in with the pour, but that was all. The architect did not want kickers for the walls or columns but we insisted on them, in order to align the shutters. The 35N concrete was probably not adequate for producing a blemish free concrete finish, but that is what was specified. We took advice from a concrete consultant on the mix design and adjusted the fine content. A water reducing admixture was incorporated in the mix and 'chemlease' release agent used on the 'Pourform' shutter panels that were purchased for the fair-face finish to the walls. The use of release agent on the 'Pourform' might have contributed to the blemishes and temporarily dusty surface, as we now know that this shuttering comes with an impregnated release agent.

The walls were braced with RMD strongbacks and the columns were formed using a fibreglass-lined box. The architects wanted us to cast the ground floor columns in one piece but there was so much rebar congesting the column that we could not get the concrete into the middle of the column – the laps took up so much space. We decided to use couplers to eliminate the laps and

Constructing meeting house elevation.

The attic studio and north
light windows.

also adjusted the concrete mix and used smaller 10 mm
rather than 20 mm aggregates. Although we subcontrac-
ted the concrete work to Donart Design – they had done
the concrete work on the British Embassy – we felt we
were not getting the best from them. When we came to
casting the concrete in the attic space, we decided to
impose a lot more supervision and control on Donart's
output. If we were to construct the Ark again, we would
prefer to do the concrete work ourselves. We would prefer to use 'Visaform' shutters not 'Pourform' and once
again use 'chemlease' release agent, which gives a very
consistent finish. The cement content of the mix would
be increased to above 350 kg/m^3 to ensure there is adequate cement paste in the mix to give an even spread of
surface colour.

Client: Temple Bar Properties
Ltd (Martin Drury, project
executive)
Architects: Shane O'Toole
and Michael Kelly/Group 91
Architects
Historic Building Consultant:
David Slattery
Structural Engineer:
KLM Carl Bro
Quantity Surveyor: Seamus
Monahan & Partners
Acoustic Consultant:
Arup Acoustics
Theatre Consultant:
Maurice Power
Artist: James Scanlon
Main Contractor:
P. Rogers & Son Ltd
Concrete Work:
Donart Design

Useable Floor Area: 1,600 m^2
Project Value: IEP 3 million
Construction Phase:
20 months
Completion: 1996

Useful Contacts

Christian Justesen
Aalborg Portland
Rordalsvej 44
Postbuks 165
DK 9100 Aalborg
Denmark

Martin Clarke
British Cement Association
Century House
Telford Avenue
Crowthorne
GB Berkshire RG11 6YS
England

Jörg Fehlhaber
BDZ
Haus am Kurplatz
Luisenstrasse 44
D 10117 Berlin
Germany

Hans Köhne
Marketing Department
ENCI
Postbus 3223
NL 5203 De 's- Hertogenbosch
Holland

Jef Apers
Febelcem
Rue Voltastraat 8
B 1050 Bruxelles
Belgium

Julio Vaquero
Instituto Espanol Del Cemento Y Sus Applicaciones
c/ José Abascal, 53 – 2º
E 28003 Madrid
Spain

Colm Bannon
Irish Cement Ltd
Stillorgan Road
Stillorgan
Co Dublin
Ireland

David Bennett
David Bennett Associates
11 Staffords
GB Harlow CM17 OJR
England
tel + 44 1279 439562
email: bencross@btinternet.com

Selected Bibliography

Appearance Matters 1: Visual Concrete Design and Production, W. Monks, BCA second edition, UK, 1988.

Aauberlingen Voor Schoon Beton, ENCI, Holland, 's- Hertogenbosch, 2001.

Beton-Atlas, Bundesverband der Deutschen Zementindustrie e.V., Friedbert Kind-Barkauskas, Bruno Kauhsen, Stefan Polónyi, Jörg Brandt, Institut für Internationale Architektur-Dokumentation, München and Beton-Verlag, Düsseldorf, 1995. (New edition Birkhäuser – Publishers for Architecture, Basel, 2001).

Betonelementbyggen, Betoncement – Foreningen, Denmark, 1991

Beton-Praxis: Ein Leitfaden für die Baustelle, Bundesverband der Deutschen Zementindustrie e.V. (ed.), Edwin Bayer, Rolf Kampen, Verlag Bau +Technik, Düsseldorf, 1986, 8th rev. ed. 1999.

Fassadenbuch: Architektur und Konstruktion mit Betonfertigteilen, Bundesverband der Deutschen Zementindustrie e.V., Fachvereinigung Deutscher Betonfertigteilbau e.V. (eds.); Wolfgang Döring, Hans-Jürgen Meseke, Friedbert Kind-Barkauskas, Dieter Schwerm, Verlag Bau +Technik, Düsseldorf, 2000.

L'Aspect Exterieur Du Beton: Dossier Cement, Bulletin 22, J. Apers, Febelcem, Belgium, 2000.

Schoon Beton, VNC, Holland, 's- Hertogenbosch, 1990.

Technical Report 50: Guide to Surface Treatments for Protection and Enhancement of Concrete, Concrete Society, UK, 1997.

Technical Report 52: Plain Formed Concrete Finishes, Concrete Society, UK, 1999.

List of Abbreviations

BS British Standard
CFC Chloro-Fluoro-Carbons
F1, F2, F3 Finish 1, 2, 3 – classifications of surface finish
GGBS Ground Granulated Blastfurnace Slag
GRP Glassfibre Reinforced Plastic
MDF Medium density fibreboard
NBS National Building Specification
OD Ordinance Survey
OPC Ordinary Portland Cement
PC Portland Cement
PFA Pulverised Fuel Ash
RMD Rapid Metal Developments
SAP – Standard Assessment Procedure (for Energy Rating of Dwellings)

Illustration Credits

Ove Arup: 40 top, 42, 43 bottom
Bastin + Evrard: 116
David Bennett: 97 top, 99 centre right, 100 left, 112 bottom right, 119 bottom right, 124 top left, 125 bottom, 126 right, 127
BIM: 96 bottom, 97 bottom, 99 bottom
Hélène Binet: 47 left
Richard Bryant/Arcaid: 44, 46
Carl Dahmen: 52–57
Dennis Gilbert: 45, 50
Benn Deceuninck: 124 top right, 125 top left
Peter Durant Images: 30–33
Thomas Ebner: 64 top, 65 top left + right, 67 top right, 68
Pablo Gallego Picard: 48 top left
Henry Gebauer: 64/65 bottom, 66 left, 66/67 centre, 68
M. Grohe: 67 bottom right
Klaus Kinold: 122/123, 123 top, 124 bottom, 125 top right, 126 left
Dieter Leistner: 58–63
Duccio Malagamba: 130 bottom, 134 top left + right, 135
Pedersen, Pedersen, Pedersen: 88–93
Peri GmbH: 2, 69 top
Paul de Prins: 114, 115, 117, 118, 119 top + bottom left, 121
Michael Reisch: 70–75
Christian Richters: 94, 95, 98 top left, 98/99 top, 100 right, 101, 102–107
Margherita Spiluttini: 48 top right, 49
Ronnie Tallon: cover photograph
Verlag Bau + Technik: 76–81
Nigel Young: 19–23, 24–29, 38 bottom, 39 bottom, 40 bottom, 41, 43 top

All images were provided by the architects and contractors involved. Photo credits are given where the photographer was made known to the publisher.